KEY TO SECTIONAL PLAN OF THE "QUEEN MARY."—(Continued.)

119. Bar.
120. Private Dining Rooms.
121. Restaurant.
122. Private Dining Rooms.
123. Foyer.
124. Third-Class Dining Saloon.
125. Third-Class Entrance.
126. Third-Class Accommodation.
127. Capstan Gear and Crew's Space.

"D" DECK.

128. Crew.
129. Suites and Bedroom Accommodation.
130. Baggage Lift Well.
131. Suites and Bedroom Accommodation.
132. Tourist Staircase and Lifts.
133. Suites and Bedroom Accommodation.
134. Stores Entrance.
135. Ice-Cream, Butter and Milk.
136. Fruit-Ripening Room.
137. Fruit Stores.
138. Vegetable and Salad Room.
139. Fresh and Frozen Fish.
140. Butcher's Shop and Meat Store.
141. Poultry, Game, etc.
142. Bacon and Eggs.
143. Grocery Store.
144. Hospital.

146. Dispensary.
147. Printers' Shop.
148. Third-Class Accommodation.
149. Oil-Filling Station.
150. Third-Class Accommodation.
151. Dressing-Rooms of Swimming-Pool.
152. Swimming-Pool.
153. Kosher Kitchen.
154. Third-Class Kitchens.
155. Third-Class Accommodation.
156. Crew.

"E" DECK.

157. Crew.
158, 159, 160, 161. Suites and Bedroom Accommodation.
162. Third-Class Accommodation.
163. Mail Discharge Room.
164. Specie Room.
165. Crew.

"F" DECK.

166. Tourist Baggage Room.
167. Bedroom Accommodation.
168. Tourist Swimming-Pool.
169. Beer Stores.
170. Lift Well.
171. Wines and Minerals.
172. Garage.
173. Registered Mail.

"G" DECK.

174. Baggage.
175, 176. Mails.
177. Linen Store.
178. Baggage.
179. Mail Space.

MACHINERY AND HOLD.

180. Rudder.
181, 182. Propeller, Starboard Side.
183. Shafts and Shaft Tunnels.
184. After Engine Rooms.
185. Forward Engine Rooms.
186. Fan Rooms.
187. No. 4 Boiler Room.
188. Air-Conditioning Plant.
189. After Turbo-Generator Room.
190. Power Station.
191. No. 3 Boiler Room.
192. No. 2 Boiler Room.
193. Forward Turbo-Generator Room.
194. Power Station.
195. No. 2 Boiler Room.
196. No. 1 Boiler Room.
197. Fan Rooms.
198. Water-Softening Machinery.
199. Tanks.
200. Baggage.
201. Mail Space.
202. General Cargo.
203. Double Bottom.

QUEEN MARY

The Scots at Sea

BBC Scotland

The Scots
at Sea

CELEBRATING SCOTLAND'S
MARITIME HISTORY

Compiled by
JIM HEWITSON

SAINT ANDREW PRESS
Edinburgh

First published in 2004 by
SAINT ANDREW PRESS
121 George Street
Edinburgh EH2 4YN

ISBN 0 7152 0811 X

British Library Cataloguing in Publication Data
A catalogue record for this book is available from the British Library

Typeset by Waverley Typesetters, Galashiels
Printed and bound in the United Kingdom by The Bath Press, Bath

Contents

Introduction: Salt in the Blood   ix

1. Whalers and a Polar Adventure   1

2. Building the Great Ships   35

3. Harvesting the Oceans   69

4. The People's Ocean   99

5. Men o' War and Safe Havens   121

6. Steamboats, Puffers and Blockade-busters   153

'The Rising Wind' by Montague Dawson, by courtesy of Felix Rosenstiel's Widow & Son Ltd., London.

Salt in the Blood

Scotland's coastline, including its islands, is approximately 18,500 kilometres in length, give or take a few rocky outcrops and forgotten lochans; a remarkable fact when you consider that the North Sea coast of Belgium is a modest seventy kilometres. Even a cursory glance at the nation's map shows the contrast between Scotland's western and eastern coasts. It could scarcely be more marked. A thousand sea lochs and as many islands bejewel the west (and north) coast while to the east, except for a few lonely outposts such as the Bass Rock, the water margin is generally uniform and clean-edged even where the great firths of Moray, Tay and Forth push into the landmass.

It is natural that a nation where everyone lives within forty-five miles (and mostly within ten miles) of salt water should have an ancient, extensive and fascinating connection with the sea. Ocean myths and saline tales abound.

Scotland's maritime history, before the Union of the Crowns, in comparison with the nation's martial exploits, is tantalisingly sketchy. Although we know that Scotland as an independent country never achieved any great naval renown, the earliest fortified coastal settlements in Scotland do suggest that her prehistoric ancestors were more-than-competent seafarers and traders. From a period not long after the end of the last Ice Age in Scotland (c. 10,000 years ago), dugout canoes have been raised from lochs and river beds. The use of these primitive yet efficient canoes persisted into the Jacobite era of the eighteenth century.

The kingdom of Dalriada on Scotland's west coast, founded by Gaelic-speaking settlers from Ulster in the sixth century AD, had a system of naval recruitment; their strength was gauged by the numbers of oars that could be manned. Feudal dues of Highland chiefs for centuries thereafter were calculated in the same way, by counting numbers of oarsmen. This clearly signals the importance of the sea to both the crown and the chieftains.

Although the sea power of the earlier Picts is by and large an unknown commodity, there is a hint that the retreating Roman legions were harried on their way by Picts and Scots who had negotiated sea lochs and rivers using wicker-covered boats called coracles. Early Christian missionaries generally travelled by boat rather than risk the wild, trackless cross-country routes.

Thereafter, the maritime connection continued. Vikings sailed the Scottish coast. They raided and encountered local opposition; but, after settling to more peaceable pursuits among the northern and western islands, they brought a style of boat-building that was to last for centuries. Robert the Bruce utilised his little fleet to keep open communications with Ireland during the Wars of Independence; Highland chieftains commanded their own war galleys; medieval Scottish traders sailed to the Baltic; and James II, in the fifteenth century, happily licensed his countrymen as privateers.

However, not until after Scotland was persuaded into a Union with England, in 1707, did her engineers, designers, merchants, shipbuilders, naval officers, maritime explorers, fishermen and ordinary seafarers begin to make their most significant contribution, within the imperialist setting.

As the industrial revolution gained momentum, by the mid-nineteenth century Scotland – and in particular Clydeside – was to become one of the world's shipbuilding capitals. In the second half of the twentieth century, this industry, like the other giants of the industrial revolution, heavy engineering and mining, gradually vanished from the scene. Into the new millennium,

Scotland's most obvious continuing links with the sea come not only through the dangerously depleted fishing industry but also through the operation of the great North Sea, and now Atlantic, oil and gas fields.

Thus, the relationship between the people of Scotland and the sea, across the centuries, has always been intimate. Reminders are everywhere, whether it's the pungent aroma of the huge fish transporters as they traverse the roads of Buchan, or the seagulls hovering above the urban motorway traffic jam in the heart of Glasgow: the sea always seems close. Trees are fine, mountains are grand, cities can be slick; but only the sea, I would contend, reaches into your very soul and whispers: 'You and I, we are of the same essence. We are one.'

It is a love affair, for sure; a coast-to-coast romance. For many, to hear the sound of the sea, to feel its eternal pulse, is as necessary as breathing. But, like every relationship, it makes demands. The sea can be reassuring, but it can also be moody and malign. I have lived on-and-off for the past twenty-five years on the Orkney island of Papa Westray. For a time, I helped work a creel boat. A quiet young man, who sailed in the little fleet from the Old Pier to fish the reefs and shelves around the island for lobster and partans, took his boat out one morning over by Weelie's Taing and never came home. He was sent to the bottom, the native islanders reckon, by the sort of rogue wave, a vast wall of water, that can suddenly rear up out of these dangerous seas.

While it is true that in the short span of a human life the great ocean can appear timeless, constant and unchanging, sea levels have been and, inevitably, will be very different from what they are today; witness the raised beaches of Argyllshire. Experts tell us that, in the Mesolithic era, not long after the retreat of the great ice sheets, the 'waist' of Scotland was as narrow as twelve kilometres, and whales swam in Stirlingshire. A land bridge linking us with Denmark, intriguingly called Doggerland, existed in roughly the same period.

This book is organised thematically rather than chronologically, and it hopes to provide an interesting sweep through some of the more significant or offbeat aspects of Scottish maritime history.

In Chapter 1, our glimpse at whaling takes us into the icy waters around both poles, first of all to the 'fishing' up by the Arctic Circle, around Spitzbergen and the Davis Strait in the eighteenth and nineteenth centuries, and then to the South Atlantic whale fishery where Britain was active until the 1960s. Whaling's vital role in oiling the wheels of Victorian industry, its rugged journeymen, the other-worldly setting, the brutal killing which depleted stocks so seriously: all of this comes under scrutiny. We'll learn that there was a 'right' and a wrong whale and a right and a wrong way to hunt them. Connections, musical and marital, between the Scottish whalers and the Inuit feature, and we find out how

Replica of the Comet.

Peterhead and Shetland benefited in turn from the two eras of whaling. Another perspective on life among the ice floes is provided in the remarkable story of Clydebank man William Laird McKinlay, who joined an ill-fated Canadian Arctic expedition in 1913.

For a century, from the 1800s, shipbuilding displayed to the world the engineering prowess of the Scots. Clyde-built warships and passenger liners dominated the oceans. In many senses, the River Clyde was where industrial shipbuilding started with Henry Bell and his pioneering steamship *Comet* and a whole succession of brilliant marine engineers and entrepreneurs. The industry produced a proud and tough breed of skilled craftsmen. Even in the 1960s and 1970s, when lack of foresight and imaginative investment saw the industry decline, these men fought to preserve a core of shipbuilding on

the Clyde in the extraordinary, mould-breaking Upper Clyde Shipbuilders work-in. Chapter 2 also reflects shipbuilding and the way in which the town of Clydebank – built initially to produce great ships – dealt with the harsh realities of world economics. Perhaps the most splendid of all sailing ships built in Scotland were the clippers of the second half of the nineteenth century that crossed the ocean to bring tea and wool to our shores. In this branch of the industry, Aberdeen played a central role.

Scotland's fishing industry is in crisis. So what's new, you might reasonably ask. It seems to have been that way for decades. The truth is that the industry has had its moments of great success but it has been dogged by the spectre of government at a distance and foreign boats on the horizon, even since the Dutch came over in vast fleets in medieval times. In Chapter 3, we focus on the dangers inherent in taking fish from the sea and the new economic pressures, the rise of the purpose-built Caithness fishing community of Pulteneytown, the way the herring industry provided a lifeline for thousands of beleaguered Highlanders in the aftermath of the Clearances, the fisher lads and lassies. The fascinating variety of boats, each adapted to particular sea and coastal conditions, comes under the microscope, as does Scotland's involvement in the Icelandic cod wars of the 1970s.

Great economic change from the late seventeenth century onwards was the main catalyst that brought hundreds of thousands of Scots into direct contact with the mighty oceans of the world through emigration. Whether fleeing poverty, cleared from their ancestral lands to make way for sheep, or leaving the dark squalor of industrial Scotland to try for a fresh start in Canada, America, Australia, New Zealand or South Africa, they took to the sailing ships and, by the 1860s, the steamships. These were the emigrants who were to become the overseas branch of the Scottish nation: the Scots diaspora. In Chapter 4, a portrayal of the great exodus is displayed by some of its component parts – the early voyages of ships such as the *Hector*, the shipboard trials and tribulations and the way in which companies such as Cunard tapped into the trade. A one-off phenomenon, the war brides of the 1939–45 conflict, constitutes a little-known element in the emigration movement.

Royal Navy connections with Scotland are very much a feature of the twentieth century reaching into this new millennium. Long-drawn-out wars with France had focused naval power in the south of England; but, as the new enemy was seen as Germany and then the Soviet Union, Scotland with its easy access to the North Sea and the Atlantic came into its own. Chapter 5 examines Scotland's medieval tour de force – the *Michael* – and considers the importance of Scapa Flow in Orkney as the fleet anchorage in both World Wars, the Battle of Jutland (the last great naval confrontation), secret west-coast training for the Battle of the Atlantic, the epic story of the Shetland Bus, and the special relationship that has developed between Scotland and the nuclear submarine fleet.

Paddle steamers and the River Clyde are synonymous. For a century and more, they crowded the Broomielaw in Glasgow, raced from pier to pier in the Firth of Clyde and provided more than a fair amount of pleasure for generations of Clydesiders. By the 1960s, car ferries were the required mode of transport about the estuary. Today, the PS *Waverley* stands as the last link to the era of the paddle steamer. Clyde paddle steamers found their way around the world and played a significant part in the Second World War as well as a largely unheralded blockade-running role in the American Civil War. No voyage 'doon the watter' would be complete without venturing for a spin on board a puffer. These couthy, pocket-sized freighters and their special place in the affections of the Western Highlands and Islands all figure in our examination in Chapter 6 of steamin' down the Clyde.

This book is designed to mirror and expand on the BBC series of the same title – *The Scots at Sea* – and wherever possible we have tried to get the people involved to tell their own story. However, this remains a vast topic, and inevitably we can only focus on a few of the main aspects – whaling, shipbuilding, fishing, emigration, the Royal Navy connection and inshore traffic.

These and a great many other topics can be found in three books that I would highly recommend to the general reader. They are:

Echoes of the Sea – Scotland and the Sea, An Anthology, edited by Brian D. Osborne and Ronald Armstrong and published by Canongate of Edinburgh in 1998.

Glimmer of Cold Brine – A Scottish Sea Anthology, edited by A. Lawrie, H. Matthews and D. Ritchie and published by Aberdeen University Press in 1998.

Scotland and the Sea by James G. D. Davidson, published by Mainstream of Edinburgh in 2003.

JIM HEWITSON
Aberdeen

CHAPTER 1

Whalers and
a Polar Adventure

I n 1880, as a medical student just out of his teens, Edinburgh-born Arthur
Conan Doyle – later famous as the creator of Sherlock Holmes – signed
on the Peterhead whaling ship *The Hope* as a ship's surgeon and set off
for the Arctic. In the imagination of adventurous young nineteenth-
century Scotsmen like Conan Doyle, the romantic pull of the frozen north was
extremely powerful.

Beside log fires in the taverns of Leith, Conan Doyle would have heard
from old seafarers glorious tales of this magical, frozen seaworld far to the
north, located beyond Greenland and the ice deserts of northern Canada.
He would also have learned of the dangerous quest for the sleek monsters of
the deep. The hunting of whales, amid stunning, scintillating, other-worldly
seascapes in northern and southern oceans, is one of the most colourful
chapters in the literature of the sea. The name of *Moby Dick*, Herman
Melville's great white whale, has harpooned the imaginations of generations
of children.

In truth, romance was in rather short supply on board ship in Conan
Doyle's time. Life was harsh – cramped living conditions, wild seas, and long
hours of punishing, bloody and messy work. Conan Doyle would have treated
patients who suffered from the many life-threatening occupational hazards of
whaling: falling from the rigging, being struck by heavy weights, slipping into
the bitterly cold water. He would have treated fractures and severe cuts, and
may have performed amputations. Even scurvy persisted as a problem into the
mid-nineteenth century: in 1835, the *Viewforth* made landfall on Orkney with

only seven of her eighty-five crew members fit for duty as a result of vitamin deficiency.

Commercial whaling out of Scottish ports came in two very distinct phases, and at opposite ends of the earth. Arctic whaling began in the late eighteenth century and lasted into the early years of the twentieth century, at first to the east of Greenland and then in the more dangerous waters to the west. In the final years of this first phase, whaling was at a much-reduced level. The second phase began just before the Second World War, when the Scottish whalers set off for the distant waters of the Antarctic. This continued after the war until 1963.

Courtesy of Dundee Heritage Trust, Royal Research Ship Discovery.

The industrial revolution kick-started many aspects of marine development, including the frantic search for whales, as their oil was an essential ingredient of economic progress. The whaling industry was lubricating the great engine of the Victorian economy. Whale oil had been important in the sixteenth and seventeenth centuries in the manufacture of paint, candles and soap; but, by the nineteenth century, with new mills, factories and machines constantly coming on stream, and before the exploitation of mineral oils such as petroleum and paraffin, there was a desperate need for the oil of the sea giants. Lubricant was needed, quite literally, to oil the wheels of nineteenth-century industry and for fuelling factory lamps so that work could continue through the hours of darkness. The earliest street lamps had also been whale-oil-fuelled, as were lighthouses and domestic lamps. The bright yellow flame was clean and virtually smoke-free.

The Dundee jute industry is an example of the close relationship between whaling and the industrial revolution. Dundee had been a leading Scottish whaling centre since the late eighteenth century – the auxiliary steam whaler was developed here – but Dundee is more famous for its jute industry. In textile manufacturing, brittle and dry fibres can cause the thread to break. According to Professor Tom Devine, Dundee was first to solve this problem by applying a mixture of whale oil and water to the fibres, a process known as 'batching' (*The Scottish Nation 1700–2000*, Penguin, 1999). Dundee was the longest-surviving of the Scottish Arctic whaling ports. It operated into the twentieth century, but it was geared to the local market connected to the jute industry.

A good many domestic items in the nineteenth century also depended very heavily on the processing of the whale. Umbrella spokes, coach springs and even ordinary hand brushes or brooms were often made from baleen fibres that hang from the upper jaw of the baleen whales and filter their food. In essence, it was like an early form of plastic – strong, light and flexible. Baleen could sell for £2,000 per ton, and even the shavings were not wasted (the inside edge of the long thin baleen plates had long bristles): these were used to stuff the seats in early railway carriages. Many garments were also reinforced with baleen. Its most notable use was, perhaps, in corsetry. Ladies' fashion of the times demanded

'New machine for winding up the ladies', c. 1828.

A CORRECT VIEW OF THE NEW MACHINE FOR WINDING UP THE LADIES

Jawbone, North Berwick Law.

elegant, pinched waists, and nothing seemed to compress the midriff better than climbing into a framework of whalebone sewn into fabric which was then laced up with appropriate ferocity by a helping pair of hands. These armour-plated pieces of underwear then accentuated narrow waists and full bosoms.

Whale-catching had been, for many centuries, a traditional feature of coastal life in Britain, particularly in the north of Scotland. The most common early technique was to *ca'* or drive the huge schools of smaller pilot whales, sometimes several hundred strong, into sheltered coves where they were beached and slaughtered. This unusual harvest formed an important, if unpredictable, element in the economy of many small communities. In Orkney, the story is told of a farmer on the island of Westray who was busy making a coffin for his recently deceased wife when the cry went up: 'Whales in the bay!' The laird was quickly on the scene but expressed surprise to see the farmer turn out for the *ca'in* on such a sad day. The response spoke volumes about the relative importance of two events: 'Ah couldna afford to lose baith wife and whales on the same day', the farmer declared earnestly.

Scottish deep-sea whaling really got under way in earnest in 1750, when the first ship sailed from Leith; business soon gained momentum. Long voyages – around Greenland, to Iceland, to Spitzbergen and to northern Canada – were necessary to reach the locations where the whales were found in the greatest numbers during their annual migrations from the cold feeding grounds in the north to the warm breeding grounds further south.

A large ship, capable of carrying a small fleet of whalers that could be launched into the sea to chase the quarry, was required. A big crew – particularly of able oarsmen – was also needed, because each whaler needed six men.

Whale arches

The price of whale oil in the nineteenth century varied between £20 and £60 per barrel as it became more scarce. Most working men would have had to labour for half a year to earn that amount of money. Whaling, although requiring initial capital funding, quickly became a highly profitable business for the ship-owners. The most lucrative years appear to have been in the 1830s when Hull, with a fleet of around fifty whalers, earned £318,000 in one season. Whale arches are a feature of the Scottish landscape that Scots of the twentieth century took somewhat for granted. Most noted, perhaps, is the great jawbone on North Berwick Law in East Lothian. But they were not merely romantic souvenirs akin to sporting trophies. Every ounce of the whale was a precious resource. The whale jaw is very spongy and saturated with oil. On board ship, after flensing – stripping down the whale carcass – the jawbone was lashed to the rigging, and the oil from the butt of the jaw was slowly drained into a barrel over a period of weeks. Extracting every last ounce from the whale made economic sense, and thus the great jawbones found their way back to Scotland. In Dundee, the **crang**, the remains of the whale blubber after it was boiled to extract the oil, was sold as manure to local farmers.

Substantial funding was essential; but, as this was not always available, not every large fishing port became a whaling port. Whaling was concentrated in Stromness, Aberdeen, Leith, Peterhead, Kirkcaldy and Dundee in Scotland, and London, Hull and Whitby in England. At least half of the whalers sailing from Britain set off from Hull.

Dr Robert Prescott, the director of the former St Andrews Institute of Maritime Studies, explains that Scotland's whaling fleet was small compared with that operating out of Hull, but the Scottish contribution was significant in other ways:

Hull and London had very much larger whaling fleets than any Scottish port. But the Scots were masters of the craft and, towards the end of the period of the Greenland whale-fishing (at the start of the twentieth century), they were also masters of the design and building of the whale-fishing vessels. The building of the auxiliary steam whaler, another Scottish development, made places like Dundee very famous because they allowed the continuation of whale-fishing long after it might have become uneconomical under the use of sail alone.

(BBC interview 2003)

Aspects of the Greenland whaling

Masters of the Greenland whalers played a vital role in the history of exploration in the Arctic, as did their successors in the South Polar Seas. Each ship had a crew of around forty to fifty men, each with a highly specialised role. It took about four years to train a harpooner. Voyages were eventually among the longest in maritime history, with overwintering quite common. Men expected to be away from home for a long time, possibly years; but the incentive for the crew was that they shared in the income from the catch. Whaling voyages generally lasted from spring to autumn, moving forwards in pursuit of the whales along the edge of the pack ice. Conditions could be appalling, with condensation freezing in the cabins just six feet from the stove.

Whaling ships had to be extremely sturdy. Even in summer conditions, they might become 'nipped' or caught in the broken Arctic ice. Many ships were crushed and totally destroyed, and the crews had to be rescued and accommodated on other vessels. When ships became trapped, the first task

> ### The 'right' whale
>
> The right whale, also known as the bowhead whale, got its name because it was more placid than the larger whales. Because of its high fat content, it floated after it was killed, and it could be towed back to the ship without further ceremony – it was the right whale to catch. Other species sank into the depths. To get round this problem, a technique was developed in the 1860s whereby compressed air was pumped into the corpse so that the whale would float until it was taken on board.

Setting sail

A party, more akin to a glorious booze-up, took place just before the ships set sail from the whaling ports. Several ships would often leave port together. Traditionally, crew members would spend their foyet (money donated by the skipper for one final fling) before catching the tide. The men drank from barrels labelled, for example, 'Knock Me Down', 'Flare Up' and 'Samson', all of which had a distinctive kick. Ribbon garlands and favours made by their womenfolk would be given to the men and would be tied to the ship's mast. The vessels leaving Peterhead usually set off around the beginning of March and headed first of all for Lerwick in Shetland or Stromness in Orkney to bring the crew up to complement. The hardy men from the Northern Isles were skilled, reliable and uncomplaining mariners even in the toughest of conditions and had sailed with mainland crews since the earliest days of commercial whaling, often demanding less money than their mainland counterparts.

was to set up an ice camp so that, if the ship were lost, the whale-catching boats would be secure to make the escape and there would be adequate food stocks. Occasionally, crews would set bonfires to thaw the ice in an attempt to free the ship. Hunting expeditions across the ice were commonplace and important in these situations to bring fresh meat to the overwintering crew and, it was hoped, to hold the curse of scurvy at bay. Canny ship-owners never supplied more than one season's food. A wary lookout for polar bears was always mounted because they were drawn from many miles away by the intense smell of the blubber.

It became common to set up whaling stations on remote headlands and inlets to gather stores for the return of the ships from whale-hunting in the open ocean. Inuit were employed to catch walrus, polar bears and seals. The advent of the auxiliary steam whaler meant that a ship could get out of trouble more easily, following a 'lead' through the ice, whereas a sailing ship might have been stranded awaiting a favourable breeze.

The great chase

Life on these whaling expeditions, which continued in Arctic waters into the twentieth century, could be harsh. Survival was often the only reasonable ambition. Thick fogs blanketed the waters where the Arctic currents met the Gulf Stream, and the whalers were easily separated from the mother ship. However, one of the most dangerous features was in the whale-catching itself. When the whale came up for air, it would be cornered against the ice edge or in an ice bay. Six men took off from the mother ship in a twenty-five-foot-long open rowing boat in pursuit of the whale, ran as close to the creature as possible and, while plunging through the waves, waited for the moment to send a harpoon arcing into the great sleek body. The whaler then ran a serious risk of being overturned by the whale's frenzied reaction to the harpooning.

Royal Navy rowing boats are still known as whalers. Thousands of soldiers were rescued from the beach at Dunkirk in 1940 by Royal Navy whalers from the destroyers which led the evacuation effort.

The hand-held harpoon was, in a sense, simply a fishing hook, not intended to kill the whale. The creature would dive deep and then exhaust itself by dragging four or five boats at the end of a couple of miles of rope before eventually resurfacing. Then it would be killed with long lances before being towed back to the mother ship. The advantage in the battle between man and the whale swung away from the great creatures in the mid-nineteenth century with the introduction of the explosive harpoon, invented by a Norwegian, Sven Foyn.

After the whale was lashed alongside, *spectioneers* (a Dutch word; many foreign words, relating to whaling, found their way into the English language), wearing spikes on their boots, would cross the slippery carcass to peel back the blubber in preparation for hauling on board. This *flensing* (a Danish word), or stripping down of the enormous whale carcass, was difficult and dangerous work. The blubber made the deck slippery underfoot, and one stumble might mean a fatal drop into the icy waters. Unlike American boats, where the boiling was done on board, the Scottish boats brought the blubber home for boiling.

Whale-fishing inevitably threw up some genuine characters. One such was William Penny, from North-East Scotland, who could be described as a pioneer whaler. He was the first man to get two seasons out of Arctic voyages. He was one of the enterprising individuals who spent a lot of time among the Inuit people and learned their overwintering techniques. He even took his wife for a season to the Arctic. Like Sir John Ross, he also captained one of the many Arctic ships that searched for the ill-fated Franklin expedition.

Scrimshaw

'Scrimshaw' is the word used to describe both the art of carving whale teeth or walrus tusks and the finished product. Carving was an important pastime for the Scottish whalers in the long months among the ice. The worked artefacts are now much sought-after by collectors.

The comradeship of the whalers in adversity is legendary. The weather in 1830 was particularly severe, possibly some of the worst of the century. Large numbers of vessels became trapped in the ice, and nineteen were lost. Not all the crews were lost; but the beleaguered, icebound seamen had to be given sanctuary on other whalers. That, quite naturally, placed great strains on the resources of the rescuing ship.

Peterhead whaling historian Alex Buchan says that the men tried everything they knew to keep the cold at bay:

> They wore two or three woollen vests, two or three sets of longjohns, waistcoats, jackets – anything they could pile on, they would wear. I'm sure they wouldn't take them off very much. One Peterhead skipper, James Vollom, had himself a chamois-leather suit made, claiming that kept him warm.
>
> (BBC interview 2003)

Ice and fog were only two of many dangers. The Arctic adventures of the whalers always made big news back home – and, on 14 November 1907, *The Glasgow Herald* carried a report of the loss of the whaler *Windward* and the epic of survival which ensued.

One of the most interesting adventures which has befallen the Dundee whalers was heard of last night on the arrival of a number of the crew of the whaling vessel *Windward* which was wrecked on a reef near Covey's Island on June 25. The present season has been disastrous for the whaling enterprise. Fishing has been a complete failure, and the greatly diminished fleet has been again reduced in number by the foundering of the *Windward*. While engaged at the Davis Strait fishing, the *Windward* struck a sunken reef, and soon foundered. There were six boats and a number of those were fully utilised for saving the men's effects, and as many provisions as possible. An island was descried in the distance and while the ship was above water provisions were carried to land. Two days later the crew made a determined attempt to reach Ponds Bay, the men taking the oars in turns and utilising the sails with particular care. The voyage was most hazardous, and on account of the severe weather it was with great difficulty that the boats kept in touch with one another. On one occasion the boat managed by the carpenter was nearly swamped. After 10 days the boats got in touch with several Dundee whalers in Ponds Bay and these took them on board. Ten of the 50 men were brought to Dundee on board the *Balena*. The voyage in open boats is considered one of the most unique in the history of Dundee whaling.

(with kind permission of the *Herald*)

These events did not always have such a positive outcome, and risk of death was a constant companion for the men who worked the Arctic oceans. In mid-March 1836, a disturbing report reached Glasgow. The whaling ship *Mary Jane* had arrived in Stromness, Orkney, having lost twenty of her crew before leaving the ice. There were harrowing scenes at the pierhead as three more men died while being carried ashore in blankets.

Chilling out to Jimmy

Sustained contacts between the Scottish whalers and the Inuit tribes were an interesting phenomenon of the era of Greenland whaling. As a legacy of these encounters, Scottish museums have amassed one of the best collections of Inuit materials and artefacts in Europe, including a number of beautifully constructed kayaks.

Every Victorian collector wanted a *narwhal* (sea unicorn) tusk, which was said to have mystical properties – and the first of these brought back from the Arctic were extremely valuable. The Inuit were particularly interested in barter

because they were short of metal tools and nails. Tea, rum and tobacco, all carried by the whalers, were also popular.

Inuit families often sailed with the whalers. Their knowledge and skills proved to be invaluable when the ships ran into trouble. The standard of foul-weather clothing on board was also much improved, as the making of skin and hide clothing was a special skill of the Inuit people.

Tradition has it that Scottish whalers regularly took Inuit women as 'bidie-ins' or partners for the duration of the voyage. Not surprisingly, there is very little information in the public record or private journals about such arrangements. Dr Robert Prescott, for one, believes that such relationships took place:

> Whalers were no different from other seafarers in this respect. They were a long time at sea, deprived of female company. I'm sure there was a good deal of interchange of that kind.

Victorian society, not surprisingly, condemned the practice; but Scotland today celebrates its links with the Inuit. In the Canadian Arctic, there is a small

---

What's in a name?

It is now well known that 'Eskimo' is a pejorative term. The word means 'eater of raw flesh', and the Inuit, understandably, were offended. The whalers soon learned not to use it. 'Inuit', the preferred name, simply means 'the people'.

---

museum that traces the relationship between Baffin Island and Peterhead, drawing attention to similarities with Scots names. For example, the Inuit name Davidie has an 'ie' added to the end of the name just as would be done with names in the Scottish fishing communities.

Michael Doig, deputy head of Peterhead Academy, helped to arrange a trip to the north-east of Scotland in 2000 for a group of young Inuit people aged between sixteen and twenty-one. They came from the Attagoyuk School in Pangnirtung, part of Arctic Canada. The young people wanted to visit because, exactly a century before, a group of Inuit fishermen had performed a national dance at Peterhead harbour. Many people in Peterhead, at the start of the twenty-first century, were stunned to see the young people dancing to an Inuit tune that was strikingly similar to a Scottish reel and which conjured up images of country dancing among the ice floes.

The late Jimmy Shand, Scotland's godfather of soulful accordion, still has millions of fans worldwide, but among the most enthusiastic are these Inuit tribes who originally learned dances and concertina techniques from Peterhead and Dundee whalers in the nineteenth century.

Over the years, a number of Inuit were brought back to Britain; but Alex Buchan admits that the Inuit were seen by some as curiosities and were put on show:

Peterhead.

Some Inuit were brought back to Peterhead. It was a great mistake because they had no resistance to white man's disease. There are three or four Inuit buried in the old kirkyard here.

One of the most famous social 'happenings' during the era of Greenland whaling occurred in that hard year of 1830. The Baffin Fair was an event with parallels in the frost fairs of centuries past when rivers in the big British cities froze over and a carnival was held on the ice. In the case of Baffin Bay, a number of ships were marooned in close proximity to each other and, when the crews took to the ice, a wild, drunken, party atmosphere developed. Shipboard artists recorded the scenes on canvas. We hear of football matches and general fun and games on the frozen playground, Inuit joining Scot in making the best of a bad situation. Thereafter, if a ship was 'nipped', and the men went on the rum, it was said they had made a 'Baffin Fair o' it'.

Whalers in Pack Ice, *oil painting by unknown artist. Reproduced by permission of Aberdeenshire Council.*

The North-East's first oil boom

The year 1893 was highly significant in the history of Scottish whaling. In that year, Captain David Gray of Peterhead skippered the *Windward* on the last whaling expedition to the Arctic from the Aberdeenshire port. In the 1850s,

James 'Paraffin' Young, from Glasgow, had begun to develop the world's first mineral-oil industry in the Lothians, refining paraffin oil and wax from shale. The red shale-heaps to the west of Edinburgh are the remnants of this industry. Meanwhile, on the other side of the Atlantic, the first industrial oil tanker was launched in the United States of America. It had been clear since the 1880s that the Arctic whales had been effectively fished out, and mineral fuels were about to come into their own.

The island of Keith Inch at Peterhead could be reasonably described as Scotland's whaling capital in the middle years of the nineteenth century; yet, poignantly, where the once bustling streets of the whaling port stood, an oil terminal is now located. Whaling began in Peterhead in 1788, when the *Robert* set off for the northern fishing grounds; but there was a tradition of whaling already established in the town. Ships from Hull would call in looking for crew. For Peterhead itself, the whaling era reached its peak in 1851, when thirty-one ships sailed from the town with well over 1,000 crewmen on board.

For decades, whaling was the key to Peterhead's prosperity, with the large houses belonging to the skippers standing as clear evidence of the money that was finding its way into the local economy. The principal whaling families included the Grays, the Gearys and the Sutters.

Keith Inch was where the blubber, stripped from the whales in the Arctic and packed into barrels, was processed. The community had three boilyards with huge copper boilers and cooling tanks, and the whalers and their families lived in the midst of all this 'aromatic' activity. Peterhead historian Alex Buchan says:

Keith Inch.

Peterhead.

People who visit Keith Inch today can't visualise it as a residential area. At one time, there were really quite handsome houses along the front facing the harbour on Keith Inch. It was like any other fishing town, except for the smell. There they were, next door to a yard that was boiling whale blubber – the smell must have been awful. I know that no whaling development was allowed on the mainland side of the harbour, so that people couldn't be offended by the smells.

Although the town had other industries, including a rapidly developing fishing sector and quarrying, Peterhead became noted at this period as an important European whale port and for the construction of whaling ships. Despite the eventual limitations imposed by the size of the harbour, more than twenty-five vessels were launched from the town's shipyards.

> Peterhead claims the biggest seasonal whale catch for a single ship ever made in the Arctic. The **Resolution** caught forty-four whales.

Temptation to join the whaling fleet was always very strong for young men in the Peterhead area. In the nineteenth century, a farm servant could earn £5 per annum while a whaler could pocket £25 in a season. Hardly surprising, then, that many farmers' sons turned to hunting the whale while the industry flourished. A folk song called 'Farewell to Tarwathie' recalls a whaler saying his goodbyes to his home farm near Strichen. Because the work was so closely tied to the summer season, Conan Doyle, in his writing, claimed that there were men among the Aberdeenshire whalers who had never seen corn grow, men who were living in permanent winter.

Perhaps the most significant figure in the history of Peterhead whaling was David Gray, nicknamed 'The Prince of Whalers', who was the third generation of one of the most successful whaling dynasties in Scotland. A pioneer in the heyday of Arctic whaling, he was also, in 1893, the last skipper to take a whaler out of Peterhead, telling people in the town that, although he knew the whaling was finished, he just wanted to make one more trip. The expedition returned with one whale.

Gray was a first-rate naturalist, as well as a keen explorer, and brought back invaluable knowledge from the Arctic for the geographical societies. He also brought back animals from the Arctic wastes – a stuffed polar bear, now one of the glories of the Arbuthnot Museum in Peterhead, was one of his trophies.

However, perhaps the most interesting outcome of David Gray's twenty-two seasons of whale-hunting was the beginning of an understanding of the delicate balance of the ecosystem, at a time in the Victorian era when exploitation of the environment was seen as a God-given right of man. He was the whale industry's spokesman at House of Commons select committees and regularly addressed animal-rights issues. Although Gray took more seals than any other master, he was the first person to propose a closed season for seal-hunting to preserve seal stocks for the future. Writing to *The Times*, as he prepared to

Keith Inch: whale-arch impression.

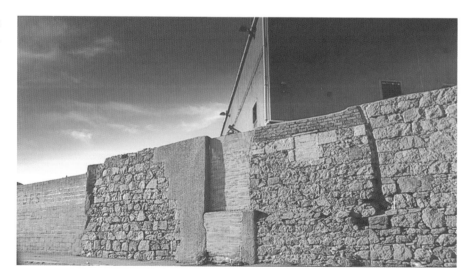

present to Parliament his case for a closed season, he declared: 'there are no greater cruelties perpetrated on the face of the globe than at the Greenland seal-fishing'.

His most noted ship was the auxiliary steam whaler *Eclipse*, which was built in 1867 by the Alexander Hall shipyard in Aberdeen. The Russians later used her as an Arctic survey vessel during the early 1900s, and she was finally destroyed during an German air raid on Archangel in 1941.

To the bottom of the world

In March 1833, when the Greenland whale fishery was still in full operation, the opening up of the Antarctic was just beginning. During that month, Scottish newspapers reported an exciting and potentially significant discovery, which at the time remained shrouded in secrecy. A whaler had 'fallen in' with a continent in the Antarctic Seas, but the owners were trying to conceal the location until they could bring off some cargoes of fur and sealskins.

The press reported that the log of the vessel was rather confused, but there seemed to be no doubt that an 'immense tract of land has been found about the latitude of 67 deg and in the longitude of the Cape of Good Hope'. The reports continued:

> It has long been conjectured that the south, like the North Pole, must have at least large islands much nearer than the adventures of any former voyages had entitled them to ascertain. Cook was of this opinion, and more recently Weddell, who penetrated so far in this direction with his merchant bark.
>
> (with kind permission of the *Herald*)

The whaling ship had indeed stumbled into the vast continent of Antarctica. A century later, the waters around this alien world were to become as familiar as the Davis Strait and Spitzbergen to a new generation of Scottish whale-catchers.

With so many whaling ships scouring the northern oceans, it had been inevitable that the whale population would decline in the Greenland fisheries. As early as the 1820s, ships, finding a dearth of whales and perhaps returning with only one creature when a few years previously they might have taken six, turned instead to seal-catching. Sealing, arguably even more bloodthirsty than whaling, was less hazardous. Whalers were forced to venture further and further into the Arctic in pursuit of their quarry, as far as the Davis Strait and the Hudson Bay.

Between 1719 and 1915, the British and Dutch took something like 120,000 bowhead whales from Spitzbergen and from the Davis Strait. Today there are probably fewer than twenty bowhead whales around Spitzbergen and a few hundred in the Davis Strait. Aberdeen University zoologist Dr Martyn Gorman does not believe that these whales, fished so mercilessly for two centuries and more, are on the road to extinction, but acknowledges the environmental damage:

> I think there is every probability that the bowhead whale will recover; but the fact that we haven't hunted it since around 1900, and we're still talking of only a few hundred or a few tens left, does show you how very slow this recovery is and how very long periods of time are needed for it to recover … Whaling was a very barbaric pursuit and it did really nothing but harm to the Arctic ecosystem.

(BBC interview 2003)

Courtesy of Dundee Heritage Trust, RRS Discovery.

This shortage of whales, in turn, led directly to the opening of the great Southern Ocean whale fishery in 1904. Dundee whalers, powered by sail, went to the Antarctic in the early years, but steam-driven ships with explosive harpoons were soon to dominate. The effort that went into improving the whaling ships is evidence of the importance of whaling to the Scottish economy. Shipbuilders and designers learned how to fortify hulls to withstand the pressure of the ice pack, and how to sharpen the bows to force their way through the ice floes. The city of Dundee, and Stephen's Yard in particular, had a special reputation, mainly because they wisely stuck with wooden-hulled barques when other fleets (including Peterhead and Hull) introduced iron steamers which were easily crushed by the ice.

This expertise was to lead to one of the city's greatest achievements – the construction of the *Discovery*, the ship that carried Captain Scott on his voyage to Antarctica. At this time, polar exploration had become a scientific obsession, and the success of the Scottish whaling fleet caught the eye of Victorian adventurers.

Whaling ships and their masters played an important part not only in the contribution that they made to the nineteenth-century economy but also in the history of exploration, contributing to the scientific interests of the nation.

So, when the Royal Geographical Society and Robert Falcon Scott were planning their first Antarctic expedition, they turned to Stephen's Dundee shipyard. The *Discovery* is the last of the line of Arctic whalers and was constructed specially to be suitable for carrying out scientific research, and she was one of the last wooden three-masted ships to be built in Britain.

The ship's hull was designed to withstand the pressure of the ice. Sea temperatures of −50°C would make iron rivets shatter. The *Discovery*, and other whalers, were made entirely of wood,

Courtesy of Dundee Heritage Trust, RRS Discovery.

with their hulls double-planked along the water-line. David Henderson of Dundee Museum has said that '*Discovery*'s bow is believed to be solid wood for about twenty feet'.

Her launch in 1901, and her famous adventures in the icy waters of the South Atlantic, secured her – and Dundee – a place in the history of polar exploration. She lies today at Dundee just a few hundred yards from where she was built, and is one of the country's major tourist attractions.

Mechanised whaling in the southern waters was quickly established. By the 1930s, over three-quarters of the world's whale catch came from Antarctic waters. This represented an average of something like 30,000 whales annually in that period.

On board RRS Discovery. *Courtesy of Dundee Heritage Trust.*

Stern of RRS Discovery.
Courtesy of Dundee
Heritage Trust.

Unilever and Salvesen were the only two whaling companies from the United Kingdom operating in the Antarctic. They turned to the new fishery when it became obvious from 1945 that Arctic whaling had ceased to be commercially viable.

Christian Salvesen, based at Leith, on the Firth of Forth, was an important Scottish shipping company founded by the descendants of nineteenth-century Norwegian immigrants. They were concerned principally with merchant shipping but, in 1907, they ventured into whaling. Large factory ships, with whale-catchers scurrying around them, were the norm in the southern oceans after the Second World War. One 30,000-ton Russian factory ship would have

Science equipment. Courtesy
of Dundee Heritage Trust,
RRS Discovery.

dwarfed the 400–600-ton whalers of the early years of the twentieth century. Unlike their sailing-ship predecessors of the nineteenth century, there was seldom any threat of the whalers becoming stuck in the ice. These twentieth-century vessels could power into the wind to make an escape if necessary.

The rugged, snow-capped island of South Georgia was chosen as a convenient location for whaling stations. Leith Harbour in South Georgia became the base of operations. Ex-whalers remember it as resembling a Wild West frontier town, but without the women. Some crewmen who worked on the whale-catchers signed contracts for twenty-two months including a winter stop-over; and, in the late 1950s, others might pick up

*Discovery Quay, Dundee.
Courtesy of Dundee Heritage
Trust.*

£300 for seven months' work plus a bonus depending on the number of whales caught. Once again, Orcadians and Shetlanders, who time and again during the first phase of whaling in the Arctic had proved themselves adept at dealing with the harsh conditions, were at the forefront of activity.

Shetland whaler Mitchell Arthur was at the Antarctic whaling from 1954–63, including overwintering at Leith Harbour. During that period, the 400 men who stayed on helped with various jobs such as overhauling the whale-catchers. There were two dry docks. In the whaling season, he had several different jobs including cutting up blubber and feeding it into the kettle, which was effectively a steam pressure cooker. The kettles on the Antarctic factory

Funnel on the RRS Discovery.
*Courtesy of Dundee Heritage
Trust.*

Anchor. Courtesy of Dundee Heritage Trust, RRS Discovery.

ships produced 85lb/square inch pressure. The tops of the cookers were level with the main deck and went down twenty-five or thirty feet into the body of the ship. At sea, the men were constantly aware of the danger around them. Says Mitchell:

> In those temperatures, if you fell overboard you were dead within four minutes; that's if your heart didn't stop with the shock as soon as you hit the water. There was no roof over the whalers. We would climb up the rigging for an hour in the crow's nest, dressed for the conditions – warm clothes, leather boots, woollen mittens underneath rubber ones. On deck, there was steam rising from the kettles, like a mist. There were wires everywhere and lumps of meat and bone; the deck was slippery with blood. The smell at times was overpowering, clinging to your clothes. You never got rid of it even when you washed them at home. If you were coming in on a catcher, you could smell the factory ship before you saw it.
>
> (BBC interview 2003)

Another ex-whaler, George Cummings, secretary of the Salvesen Ex-Whalers Club, recalls:

> Conditions in the station were better than on board the factory ship. The accommodation could be built away from the work area. On the ship, there was no escape from the noise and smell.
>
> (BBC interview 2003)

Throughout the day, every effort was made to ensure that there was a steady flow of whales back to the factory ship, and sometimes there might be whales moored around the factory ship waiting for processing. Deckhands would line the whales up for processing, and winches pulled them into the ship through a great opening in the stern of the vessel. This opening was given many names, 'Hell's Gate' being one of the more descriptive. It was not uncommon to see men up to their knees in whale flesh as the flensing continued.

George worked in the South Atlantic during the early 1960s until the last British whale factory ship, the *Southern Harvester*, was sold in 1963 when Britain abandoned whaling permanently. George was a deck labourer working a twelve-hour day, but points out that he was substantially better paid at that time than a building-site labourer.

> To this day, Scotland's Antarctic connection is maintained in a rather novel way. Lord Salvesen was the first chairman of Edinburgh Zoological Gardens, and the company's presence around the ice continent resulted in the Zoo's world-famous collection of penguins.

Whaling-station life must certainly have been a more attractive option. On board ship, the men were thrown about in bad weather, they sometimes had to sleep in their oilskins and there was the constant realisation that just beyond the thin metal bulkhead lay what could be the wildest ocean on the planet. Mitchell Arthur remembers that work on the catchers started at 6 a.m. and they were often still busy at 11 p.m.

Gibbie Fraser, of West Burrafirth in Shetland, is the third generation of his family to have gone to the whaling. In 2001, he compiled an oral history book, *Shetland's Whalers Remember*, which contains the recollections of fifty men who went to the Antarctic fishing grounds in the twentieth century. He notes that a special bond developed among the whalers as they worked in the hostile conditions at the bottom of the world.

Salvesen had a base in Shetland and became familiar with the way in which Shetlanders worked. The Antarctic whaling tied in well with the crofting way of life. Hundreds of Shetlanders could go to the whaling from September to

May and still be home in time to cut the peat, bring in the harvest or go to the herring-fishing in the summer. Whaling became an important element in the Shetland economy.

Excitement took sixteen-year-old Gibbie to the whaling as a deck mess and galley boy. After a testing first twenty-four hours of seasickness on the whale-catcher, he warmed to the work, finding both the excitement he had craved and the sense of purpose and comradeship which went with the quest for the whale. 'The danger was like a drug', he confesses. Gibbie remembers the storms of the Roaring Forties (referring to a latitude of forty degrees) and the bloodbath that was the deck of the factory ship:

> It was a vision of hell – a red, oily mess. I felt sorry for the whales. They were on the brink of extermination. Even in the four years I was there, you could see a decline in the numbers. It's not a job I'd like to do now.
>
> (BBC interview 2003)

Looking back over his period in the Antarctic, Mitchell Arthur also has regrets about the killings. He recalls in particular the day they shot a female humpback whale but she didn't die. Other whales, including her pup, turned back to see what had happened, and one after another they were killed. Twenty-five whales were shot that day. Good bonus money, of course; but, as the whaler admits:

> It was sheer butchery. When you think back, no animal on earth deserves to die the death that those poor creatures did. Looking back, we almost fished the poor animal to extinction.

Memories of shipboard life for Gibbie centred on the fresh bread every day, the good pay without anywhere to spend it, the whales, and of course the spectacular Antarctic scenery. Going into the Antarctic seas with the whale-catcher, they soon encountered the floating islands of ice:

> The icebergs were fantastic shapes, pieces were falling off, or they were rolling over. They were mostly white although occasionally dark green or blue. I even saw black ice once. And the sea ate ice caves in the side of the bergs. We were never out of sight of the ice. There were always icebergs around and they varied from little bits the size of your fist up to islands, oh, maybe fifty or sixty miles long. As the large ones broke up, you got those weird shapes, faces, profiles.

If the weather deteriorated, the catcher would try to get into the lee of an iceberg. As Mitchell Arthur observed: 'If it was rough, the ice could protect or kill'. Memories of the wild ocean have stayed with Gibbie Fraser for fifty years:

> While we were coming in that very last season, we were hit by a terrible storm – the worst seas I've ever seen. One big wave engulfed our catcher. We just seemed to vanish for a while, the bridge and the funnel was all that seemed to be up, and then she slowly shook herself clear and came up again. Everybody was standing on the bridge with their thoughts. Nobody said anything. We all stood very quietly until it cleared.

The true remoteness of their location generally only came home to the whalers when someone took ill or was injured. During one of Gibbie Fraser's sojourns in the south, one young Norwegian developed polio and the engineers devised an iron lung for him. The company was always reluctant, because of the cost, to ship people out. Gibbie was involved in taking a man who had been run over by a tractor from Leith Harbour to the Falkland Islands, but the injured man was only permitted this concession because it was not during the whaling season.

A very efficient catching and processing system soon developed in the South Atlantic. The 'catcher boats' normally held a crew of fifteen and were about 160 feet long. The buoy boat, which collected the dead whales, could tow up to twelve whales, six on each side and weighing in total up to 600 tons. The harsh conditions under which these whalers were expected to work would unquestionably have seen the operation quickly closed down today by Health and Safety regulations.

The top job on the catcher boats, as you might expect, was that of the gunner, the mid-twentieth-century equivalent of the Arctic harpoon man. Says Gibbie Fraser:

> The gunner was just like a god. The man I was with for three seasons was an absolute gentleman. He was the only one on board ship that you didn't use first-name terms with. He was The Gunner. Despite this, you were basically a team on the whale-catcher.

Priority quarry for the whale-hunters was the sperm or tooth whale – some had as many as sixty teeth – which gave high-grade oil used for margarine and soap.

By-products of this particular whale included the use of its blood for beef drinks and its meat for cattle feed. The once-prized baleen plates – from the toothless baleen whales – made from keratin, the same substance as fingernails, were by this time being dumped. The disposal of heaps of whale intestine would bring clouds of seabirds round the whaling fleet.

Gunner on board Soviet whaling ship. British Film Institute – ETV Collection.

As more and more sophisticated tracking equipment was introduced, the odds began to stack up against the whale. The Antarctic industry was highly technological, and the same pattern of whale-depletion as in the Arctic soon became apparent: each time the hunters had fished out a particular type of whale, they moved on to smaller species. Says Dr Martyn Gorman:

> The story of the Antarctic industry was one of over-exploitation of one species after another. The whale industry was always known as a fishery, and the way that we exploited whales was exactly analogous to the way that we generally exploit fish, taking them until they are no longer economic to fish, then moving on to the next species.

Another ex-Salvesen Scot, Don Lennie, was in the Antarctic from 1956 until 1963, and recalls the strange, eerie atmosphere found at the edge of the great ice continent, the icebergs with their myriad shades and the huge monsters that were their quarry:

> On occasion, we fished right on the edge of the ice field. There we found some huge whales – eighty-four feet was the largest specimen we landed, a Blue – the biggest of the whales. Catching a whale was

an exhilarating experience. There was always someone on duty in the barrel strapped to the masthead watching for the puff of moisture as the whales breathed out. The weather was always clear and you could see for miles. I remember the day we started chasing a whale at midday and it was ten hours before we brought it to a halt. Quite impressive – an eighty-ton creature propelling itself through the water with you trailing behind. The isolation was something you got used to, but weeks without seeing a whale and everyone was down in the mouth.

The intense cold is something you never forget. I've seen a sunny day with blue, sunny skies and the temperature at minus thirty or forty degrees below. Moisture froze on our beards, ice caked on railings around the ship and the halyards grow to twice their normal thickness.

(BBC interview 2003)

These long stints in the Antarctic took their toll on the folks back home. Shetlander Betty Waters's first husband served with Salvesen on a whale-catcher whose crew were mostly Norwegian. He was away from home for nine months of the year, from August until April; if he agreed to overwinter, it was the full twenty-two-month contract. Says Betty:

I had a daughter of ten months and was pregnant when he left. My second daughter was six months old when he got back. It was very lonely when they left, but when the New Year came in you began to look forward to April. Allowances for the women were given every fortnight from their wages, then they would bring home a bonus. They would bring nice gifts from places where they stopped on the way, like Tenerife.

(BBC interview 2003)

Tough and testing though it may have been, Gibbie Fraser puts the Antarctic whaling into perspective when he admits: 'We had it soft compared to the old-time Arctic whalers. We wanted for nothing – there was even a shop on board.'

It is calculated that, between 1904 and 1963, as many as one million whales were killed. The subsequent decline of whale populations led to economic and environmental pressures, and whaling was largely abandoned. Japan is now the main deep-sea whaling country, arguing that they have a tradition of whale-hunting that stretches back 2,000 years and that the killing continues only for research purposes.

Marooned in an ice desert

The nineteenth-century adventurers, as well as providing vital navigational and weather information for those who would follow in their wake, also provided some of the earliest ethnographic information on the Inuit people whom they encountered around Greenland and Baffin Island. Not only were the whalers finding the fuel to light and grease the wheels of industry, they were also contributing to scientific understanding of a romantic, mysterious yet menacing part of the world.

Scottish-built whaling ships earned a reputation for their resilience amid the merciless ice. An historical account of Peterhead, written in 1815 by Arbuthnot, declared that there were no finer ships built anywhere in Britain and that they had achieved their fame through their superior construction which allowed them to venture into ice that defeated other ships.

At the same time as the Scottish whalers were scouring the Arctic waters, the Royal Navy was exploring the same region on map-making duties. Sir John Ross, from Wigtownshire, joined the Navy at the age of nine and served with distinction in the Napoleonic Wars. In 1818, he led an expedition in search of the Northwest Passage, and in 1850 he made an unsuccessful attempt to find the Franklin expedition (missing since 1846) that had set out with the same purpose – finding a sea route to the Far East through the Arctic extremities of Canada.

It was not only whaling which took Scots out into the frozen wastes. Many Scots joined scientific expeditions to both poles in the early years of the twentieth century. However, the story of Scotsman William Laird McKinlay is exceptional, and his connection with the ill-fated *Karluk* mission remains one of the most compelling tales of polar adventure. The fate of his crewmates haunted him for the rest of his life, and his diaries are a precious resource of early Arctic exploration.

In the years before the First World War, the area to the north of Alaska, in the Beaufort Sea, was marked on maps as 'unexplored'. Some scientists believed it to be simply part of a large northern ocean, but others felt it was quite probable that land, perhaps even a vast undiscovered continent north of the Canadian archipelago, would be found there.

A world away – at 69 Montrose Street, Clydebank, to be precise – William Laird McKinlay, a maths and science teacher at Shawlands Academy in Glasgow, opened a telegram on 26 April 1913, asking if he would take four years away from the classroom to join the Canadian Arctic Expedition.

*Armour-plated bow of the Karluk. With kind permission of
the Executors of Mrs Annie Baillie-Scott.*

Test tubes aboard the Discovery. Courtesy of Dundee Heritage Trust, RRS Discovery.

The job offered to McKinlay was that of magnetic observer; there was no salary, but all expenses were paid. Then twenty-four years old, he had, as a boy, devoured all that was to be read about polar exploration. He knew that the risks were immense.

Events unfolded rapidly. McKinlay met with the Canadian Commissioner in London and, almost before he knew what was happening, he was shipboard for Canada. The situation when he arrived on the west coast was not encouraging. Bickering between different factions was immediately obvious.

Only three months into the voyage, the *Karluk* became locked into the ice and began to drift westwards along a line roughly parallel to the north Alaskan coast. The ship faced almost certain destruction.

Opposite Point Barrow, Alaska's most northerly landfall, the current that was carrying the ship westwards met with a current flowing up through the Bering Straits from Japan. The two huge icefields came together in an awesome display of the might of nature – huge ice floes, several square miles in extent, crashing into and riding high over each other. McKinlay, in a television interview in 1980, described how huge chunks of ice the size of houses were rolling about, and remembered the remarkable sounds ranging from the merest twanging of stretching ice to the thunderous roars of collision:

> We could only hope that the centre of destruction would not reach the ship, because there was only one thing that would happen. The ship and ourselves would be engulfed beyond all hope of salvation.

(McKinlay extracts with permission of Dilwyn Jones)

The *Karluk* somehow survived this nightmare to see Christmas and the New Year. The end, however, was only delayed. On 11 January 1914, she was crushed in the ice. Twenty-five people took shelter in what they were to call Shipwreck Camp, which had been prepared on an adjacent ice floe for the inevitable loss. A rough dwelling had been built from cases and boxes. McKinlay movingly described the last hours of the *Karluk* as the pressure of the ice became too much for the old whaling ship:

I was wakened one morning by a harsh creaking sound just along-side my bunk. It sounded as if the edge of the ice was scraping along the wood of the hull … when I got to the top of the engine-room steps, I found the skipper and the chief engineer already there … there was a gap in the hull about ten feet long and the water was pouring in … the order was given to abandon ship. The captain was the only one who remained aboard. He moved the gramophone from the mess room into the galley along with a stock of records and proceeded to put on each in turn … when each one finished, he broke it over his knee and dropped it into the galley fire … He then put on the *Funeral March* and stepped on to the ice leaving the record playing. The ship went down on an even keel. We had hoisted the Canadian ensign and, as the ship settled, that was the last thing we saw of her, the ensign spread on the surface of the water.

The loss of this fragile sanctuary from the elements had a profound effect on the physical and mental health of the party. During the long months that followed, the survivors struggled first to reach the bleak, icebound Wrangel Island and then to keep themselves alive there. The party split into groups in order to maximise the hunting opportunities for polar bear and seals. Circumstances deteriorated over the months of isolation: first of all the survivors fed the polar-bear offal to their dogs, and then they had to eat the offal themselves.

The captain headed for Siberia by dog sled to seek help; and, of the twenty-five people who had set off in the *Karluk*, eleven died in what was described as 'the

The captain of the Karluk *played the* Funeral March *as he gave the order to abandon ship.*

greatest Arctic disaster since the Franklin Expedition' (to find the Northwest Passage). Nine months after the *Karluk* vanished into the Arctic Ocean, a whaling schooner rescued the survivors from Wrangel Island as they prepared to face another Arctic winter. When McKinlay returned to Europe and the ravages of the First World War, he described life in the trenches as a blessed relief.

How did the wee man from Clydebank survive? His strong religious convictions were a major factor, and he felt strangely at home on Wrangel Island in what for most people was an extremely alien environment:

It was as like Scotland as anywhere I've seen except that there were no bushes or growth other than dwarf vegetation. But I'd only to look at these hills and I always felt at home … at peace.

McKinlay also talked, towards the end of his life, of the moments in the Arctic, staring eternity in the face, when his faith was immeasurably strengthened. He had gone out for a stroll on the ice on a beautiful moonlit night and looked back to see the ice-locked *Karluk* glistening in her frosty cloak:

And I now became aware of something strange … an awareness of a presence. It's difficult, indeed impossible to describe the feeling …

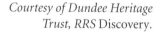

Courtesy of Dundee Heritage Trust, RRS Discovery.

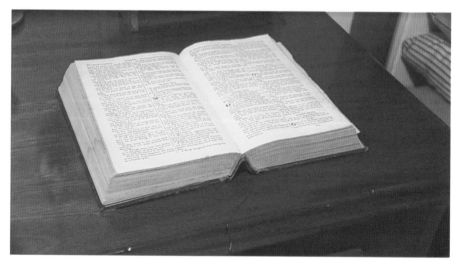

but it was enough to leave me with a firm conviction that none of
the unbelievers ... would ever deny me the right to believe in God.
As I turned, as I went towards the ship, I was overcome with a joyful
feeling.

CHAPTER 2

Building the Great Ships

The American War of Independence (1776–83) was an important factor in the development of Scottish shipbuilding. Since medieval times, wooden ships had been built on a small scale on the lower Clyde at places like Dumbarton and Greenock. Until the American War of Independence, most of the vessels on the Atlantic routes had been built in North America, taking advantage of the plentiful timber. When the Scottish merchants were no longer able to order ships from America, they began to place contracts with local yards, and the industry expanded to meet this demand.

One area of expertise in shipbuilding at this time was in the north-east of Scotland, in Aberdeen: here, in 1839, William Hall, of Alexander Hall & Son, designed the 142-ton schooner, *Scottish Maid*, with a steeply raked bow that greatly increased the speed of the ship. By the mid-1840s, fast sailing ships, which could 'clip' days off voyages and were hence called 'clippers', were being built in Scottish and in north-east English shipyards. In the mid-nineteenth century, as steam power began to transform ocean-going ships, sailing ships paradoxically enjoyed their finest hour. This became the era of the clipper, and Scotland was again at the forefront in both the construction and the crewing of these magnificent trading vessels.

Clippers were designed specially for long-distance ocean transit. They ruled the waves between 1845 and 1875, when speed was everything. They are most closely identified with the Far East tea trade and the Australian wool trade, and would regularly complete in less than 100 days journeys which, in the past, might have taken a year or more.

William Hall. Reproduced with kind permission of the Aberdeen Maritime Museum.

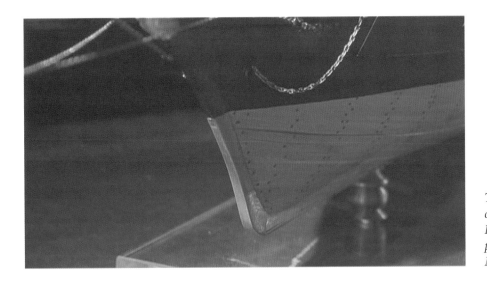

The steeply raked bow of the Scottish Maid. *Reproduced with kind permission of the Aberdeen Maritime Museum.*

The early clippers brought back tea from China. As naval architect Fred Walker points out, tea had a high value and it was also a lightweight cargo, so it paid for the voyage. Until the 1830s, the East India Company held the monopoly on the export of tea; but, after deregulation, tea companies with heavy Scottish corporate involvement began to spring up in London – for example, Jardine-Matheson, Melrose and Lipton.

Tea is a crop that is harvested annually at locations which, in the nineteenth century, were still many months' journey time away from Britain. Tea had been reaching Britain in large quantities since 1780, when the government lowered the duty payable. For the big country houses and city mansions, receiving the first of the year's crop conferred a status that they coveted. It was similar to the

Navigation equipment. Reproduced with kind permission of the Aberdeen Maritime Museum.

Fashionable tea-drinking.

way that restaurants and hotels vie in our own time to bring the first bottles of Beaujolais to the dining table.

The 1860s and 1870s are seen as the zenith of the clipper industry because, by the 1880s, more reliable ocean steamships had begun to outpace the clippers. However, the technology of the steamships was still being refined, and so the clippers were transferred to the Australian run, which remained beyond the reach of steamships because there were not enough coal refuelling points en route. An innovation in steam-engine efficiency – better high-pressure boilers to reduce the amount of coal needed – was still awaited. In this period, clippers were known as 'colonial clippers' as, on the outward leg, they often carried emigrants to a new life. Soon, just to make a living in the steam revolution, they were also carrying coal, nitrates and grain.

Vast areas of canvas sail were used on the clippers to catch as much wind as possible and to extract every last bit of speed out of the vessels. The Suez Canal is seen as having killed off the romantic, adventurous voyage around the Cape of Good Hope; but the truth is that, while the voyage to the other side of the world may have been romantic, more rational observers regarded

The Cutty Sark. *Reproduced with kind permission of www.cuttysark.org.uk*

Fife rivals in the tea race

Hundreds of adventure stories have been based around the tea clipper, but in 1866 a real-life drama eclipsed anything that an imaginative author could conjure up. The rivalry between the Fife villages of Cellardyke and Anstruther came to a spectacular public climax during the great annual tea race. Among the fifteen clippers that were to compete over the 16,000-plus miles from Foochow in China to London were the **Ariel**, *whose skipper, called Keay, was from Anstruther, and the* **Taeping**, *owned by Alexander Rodger, a native of Cellardyke. This epic contest was to end after so many hazardous miles in almost a triple dead heat, prompting observers to describe it as one of the closest races of all time – of any sort – taking more than three months to complete. The ships set off on 29 May, laden with tea, down the coast of China on a route that took them round the tip of present-day Vietnam, across to the Cape of Good Hope and north into the Atlantic. The main rival to the clippers with a Fife connection was the* **Fiery Cross**, *which got off to a flying start from Foochow but was then becalmed in the Atlantic. When the first ships appeared in the English Channel in September, the* **Ariel** *and the* **Taeping** *were matching each other wave for wave, and a smaller vessel, called the* **Serica**, *was on their tail. However, it was the* **Ariel** *which looked to have won this tightest of finishes until she drew too much water in the River Thames and was overtaken in the last few hundred yards by the* **Taeping**. *After so many miles, they docked within half an hour of each other.*

it as a severe test of seamanship. Crews had to face typhoons in the South China Sea, difficult conditions rounding the Cape, the madness of the Roaring Forties and a hundred other hazards ranging from icebergs to the nightmare of fire at sea.

Britain went wild for the tea races, and huge bets were placed on the outcome. The need, in smart drawing rooms across the land, to serve the 'new' tea became more like a fixation rather than merely a snobbish cachet. The first ship home naturally commanded the greatest premium.

The defining characteristics of the tea clipper were a sharply raked bow, an overhanging stern and acres of sail. They were also capable of prodigious

Rigging on the Cutty Sark. Reproduced with kind permission of www.cuttysark.org.uk

speeds, regularly travelling at up to eighteen knots. When you consider that a modern frigate cruises at fourteen knots, this is a stunning performance. Their hulls were narrow, which limited the carrying capacity, and the huge spread of sail needed a large crew; but speed was the compensation. Among the most famous clipper shipyards were Alexander Hall & Sons in Aberdeen, and Denny's in Dumbarton – birthplace of the *Cutty Sark*.

The *Cutty Sark*'s greatest rival was, unquestionably, the Aberdeen-built *Thermopylae*, considered by many to be the fastest tea clipper ever constructed. The vessels were very evenly matched, and both were renowned for their speed through the water. The *Thermopylae* held the record for the outward leg of the wool run from London to Sydney, a staggering fifty-nine days, while the *Cutty Sark* claimed the record for the return leg. It is said that the *Cutty Sark* was so fast that the copper sheathing was burned as she skimmed along.

One man, Hercules Linton, from Inverbervie in Kincardineshire, provides an unusual link between the two vessels. He was the designer of the *Cutty Sark* and is thought to have served his apprenticeship in Walter Hood's yard, in Aberdeen, where the *Thermopylae* was built in 1868. There is a memorial in Inverbervie to Linton, which was erected with the help of the Cutty Sark Society.

Jock Willis, owner of the *Cutty Sark*, and George Thompson junior, owner of the *Thermopylae*, were passionately committed to producing the fastest vessel. Rivalry between the yards was as intense as that between ship-owners. Aberdeen yards were generally top dogs, regularly proving themselves to be a step ahead of their Clydeside rivals in the clipper construction business. It is on record that many workers were tempted away from Aberdeen to work in Dumbarton on the *Cutty Sark*, further increasing the rivalry.

The Cutty Sark. *Engraving after a painting by Jack Spurling. Getty Images.*

This belligerence spilled over much further afield. Simon Schofield, from the Cutty Sark Trust, says that there are records of angry exchanges over the merits of the respective vessels:

> There was a violent confrontation in Portsmouth between sailors arguing the case of which vessel – the *Thermopylae* or the *Cutty Sark* – was the fastest. Sailors would be pulling knives on each other as the argument got more heated. There are echoes of this debate even today in the boating magazines.
>
> (BBC interview 2003)

Working on clippers was generally a young man's job, and many from the fishing and crofting areas signed up for a clipper adventure. Thrown together

in the cramped conditions of the fo'c'sle for months on end, it was important that men were able to work together. This was especially so when they climbed as a team high into the rigging to work with the sails.

In 1872, the *Thermopylae* left Shanghai for London with a cargo of tea at the same time as the *Cutty Sark*. After racing each other for about two weeks, the *Cutty Sark* lost her rudder and the *Thermopylae* finally arrived in London seven days ahead of her rival. The *Cutty Sark* put in some sparkling performances but was never able to outrun her Aberdeen rival; this occasion in 1872 was the only time when the two famous vessels went head to head.

The Dumbarton-built *Cutty Sark* is seen by most maritime specialists as representing the pinnacle of sailing-ship design, blending the durability of iron

and wood most successfully. Until then, American clippers had monopolised the market. The *Cutty Sark* was built in 1869, the same year as the opening of the Suez Canal, and is now permanently berthed as a major tourist attraction on the Thames, where she is held in great affection by the British public. Simon Schofield believes that she is a very special ship:

> There is definitely an aura of romance surrounding the *Cutty Sark*. She had great stamina and was ideally suited to the Australian route. She was breaking records to Australia when she was thirty years old – unusual for a sailing ship.

Although there is a secure berth for the *Cutty Sark*, named after the witch in Robert Burns's *Tam o' Shanter*, the *Thermopylae* met a sad end. She was sunk, torpedoed deliberately in 1906, by units of the Portuguese navy on target practice. The wrecks of famous clippers are still being found all across the oceans. The remains of the *Taeping* have been found in the South China Seas.

Clydeside: seedbed of industrial shipbuilding

It was not until the first half of the nineteenth century that Clyde shipbuilding grew suddenly and spectacularly to gain international stature and become a crucial component in the nation's economy. This was to be the new phenomenon of 'industrial and scientific shipbuilding', carried out on a vast scale, particularly on the upper reaches of the river. Scotland was now setting the shipbuilding benchmarks for the rest of the world.

This improvement in the Glasgow area's fortunes stems from the city's unique location: on a river estuary, on top of extensive coalfields and at the heart of a rapidly developing transport infrastructure. Glasgow became the urban core of a remarkable industrial complex. As the industrial revolution gained pace, ironworks, coalmines and engineering shops studded the Clyde Valley; the river was dredged, and the era of big ship construction on the upper reaches began.

Graham Kennison, a trustee of the Scottish Maritime Museum at Irvine, suggests that there were also other factors at work:

With kind permission of www.cuttysark.org.uk

City of Adelaide.
Reproduced by kind permission of the Scottish Maritime Museum.

These developments gave them the raw materials and the skills. But, I think, almost as significant was the fact that Glasgow was an important commercial centre where there were banks, managers, lawyers. It really gave them all they needed to produce these large, complex and expensive vessels.

(BBC interview 2003)

Following James Watt's development of the separate condenser in 1765, by 1792 steam power was first being used for spinning, and many textile mills in and around the city were soon powered by steam. It was not long before enterprising local millwrights and engineers began to apply the new technology to the problem of ship propulsion.

Scotland had become a leading entrepreneurial nation, but equally important was the fact that there was a large industrial workforce in Glasgow which was daily being boosted by new arrivals from the surrounding countryside, from the

City of Adelaide *hull.*
Reproduced by kind
permission of the Scottish
Maritime Museum.

Gaelic-speaking areas of the Scottish Highlands and from Ireland. As technical skills were honed, wooden hulls were replaced first of all by iron and then by steel. Important innovations were soon being reported locally in marine engineering, particularly in relation to propulsion. An additional blessing for Glasgow was its long-established university, which early on became involved with scientific shipbuilding and the science of ships.

Jimmy Reid, a leader of the Upper Clyde Shipbuilders work-in of 1971 (see p. 63), traces Clyde shipbuilding's advantage in part to the eighteenth century, when Scottish intellectual and scientific life blossomed. This was partly related to the fact that Scottish universities had science and engineering faculties when English universities were still concentrating on Latin and Greek. 'This diversity

City of Adelaide *hull.*
Reproduced by kind
permission of the Scottish
Maritime Museum.

The saga of the City of Adelaide

Now at the *Scottish Maritime Museum* in Irvine, awaiting funding for restoration, is the **Carrick**, the only surviving sailing passenger liner in the world. She was built in Sunderland in 1864 and was first named the **City of Adelaide**. With a grand piano in the salon, and a milk cow in the hold, she took wealthy passengers to Australia and brought back the merino wool clip. A very fine wool, the merino had to be clipped and received in Britain in the autumn so that it could be spun and woven into clothing for the Christmas market. As with the tea trade, the first cargo home got the premium prices. After ten highly profitable trips, the ship's owners sold her, and she worked as a timber ship, then as a hospital ship at Southampton, before being bought by the Royal Navy and renamed the **Carrick**. Brought to the Clyde, she served as a drill ship, guard ship and accommodation unit for the Wrens before being decommissioned and taking up a new role as the Royal Naval Volunteer Reserve club. In the late 1980s, she sank in Princes Dock in Glasgow while awaiting upgrading. She was raised over several days in 1992, using huge airbags, before being towed down to Irvine and put on to a shipyard slipway.

She was raised with restoration in mind; but the Museum had sufficient cash only for the transfer to Irvine and to make a start on restoration. Since then, the priorities of the funding bodies have changed, and another major supporter is still to be found. It may take £5–7m for a complete restoration. Graham Kennison, a trustee of the Scottish Maritime Museum at Irvine, outlines the latest grim situation: 'There's been no work of any substance now for five or six years, and this is tragic given the world significance of this vessel. She is considered one of the ten most important hulls in the world, yet she is sitting out in the weather with her timbers shrinking, her paint falling off and steadily declining into rot. As a Museum, our funding is precarious and we have to pay a rental for the slipway. She is a great drain on our resources.'

However, an English businessman, Michael Edwards, has offered money. He would have preferred the vessel to stay in public ownership; but, when it became apparent that a public rescue fund was unlikely to be forthcoming, he effectively bought the option to purchase the vessel, and his dream is to restore her to sailing condition. A feasibility study is being conducted, and Michael Edwards has given money to the Museum to secure the vessel. At the moment, a roof is being built over her and various good housekeeping methods are being brought in to try to arrest any further deterioration.

in Scottish universities engendered innovation', says Jimmy Reid. James Watt, who many agree kick-started the industrial revolution, was a technician in the University of Glasgow.

It was here that a chair of naval architecture was introduced, and this in turn led to the science of hydrodynamics. By the 1870s, William Frood was developing this discipline, and he was commissioned to construct the world's first commercial ship model test tank by the Denny shipyard at Dumbarton. Graham Kennison outlines the background:

> Before the development of scientific ship-testing, it was all really rule
> of thumb and a lot of prejudice. David Napier had actually started
> testing in the early 1800s by damming up a burn at Camlachie in
> Glasgow for his models. However, with the scientific test tank, it
> was possible to refine the hull forms not only for greater efficiency
> and speed but also for different sea conditions. So, ships could be

City of Adelaide *hull.*
*Reproduced by kind
permission of the Scottish
Maritime Museum.*

confidently built on the Clyde which were equipped for the peculiar conditions they might find, for example, in the Red Sea. The test tank enabled the shipyard to build a vessel that would meet the contract terms – and that was usually a matter of speed. But it also enabled them to do such things as stability testing, which added considerably to the safety. By putting in a wave machine, they were able to replicate wave profiles from different parts of the world. So they were able to build from Glasgow, from the Clyde, ships that could sail safely in seas anywhere in the world, and it made them an international force for scientific shipbuilding. That tank survives to this day at Dumbarton, and it is probably one of the most important buildings in the history of ship development in the world. The facility is still operated by Glasgow and Strathclyde Universities for modern testing and for student, development and commercial work.

Although there were various prototypes of steam-powered vessels built at the beginning of the nineteenth century, including William Symington's *Charlotte Dundas* and the *Vulcan*, the first properly designed iron ship and the model for all subsequent iron and steel ships, it was Henry Bell who produced the first commercially viable steamboat, the three-horsepower *Comet*. The hull was built in Port Glasgow, while the celebrated engineer David Napier constructed the boiler.

For the most part, it was local engineers and millwrights who constructed the engines for these pioneering vessels. Robert Napier, a cousin of David, was to become the chief innovator of marine engines during the first half of the nineteenth century. There had been confusion over who had constructed the prototype engine for the Clyde steamboats; so, in 1825, the Napier cousins joined others in signing a letter confirming that Henry Bell was the first to design the steam engine on which the engines of succeeding vessels were based.

Robert Napier became known as 'the father of Clyde shipbuilding' for two principal reasons. First, at Govan, he pioneered the idea of an integrated iron shipbuilding yard, engine works and foundry to deal with the much more complex business of building steamships. This meant that he had the whole shipbuilding process, including costs and quality, under his control. These changes were crucial to his success and set the standard for others to follow throughout the world. Records of actual numbers employed in the yards in those early days are scant, but it is thought that Napier may have employed up to 6,000 men at any one time. Says Graham Kennison: 'In developing the concept of the integrated shipyard, Napier really laid down a blueprint for the development of shipbuilding on the Clyde and elsewhere'.

Second, he gained the epithet from the fact that so many engineers who learned their trade under his watchful eye went on to open shipyards of their own. The list of former Napier apprentices who set up in business in their own right reads like a shipbuilders' *Who's Who*. It includes such familiar Clydeside names as Randolph and Elder, who established Fairfield's shipyard in Govan and which still exists under the ownership of BAE Systems; and also George Burton Hunter of Swan Hunter on Tyneside, as well as James and George Thomson, founders of what would later become John Brown's Shipyard at Clydebank, arguably the most famous shipyard in the world. Napier was also known as 'the apostle of reliability', and he worked hard to ensure that engineers had as much access as possible to the engine to facilitate repairs while at sea.

Jimmy Reid speaks of this sudden coincidence of 'weird engineering geniuses' beside the Clyde. And their echo persisted down the years. Says Reid:

> When I was a kid, I remember I used to read stories about the steamers in the West Indies and in every one I read there was always an old Scot, the chief engineer, who was worldly-wise. And then my kids were watching *Star Trek* and the engineer is Scottie. It's almost written into literature, this tremendous role that the Scots, and above all Clydesiders, played in developing shipbuilding, marine engineering and engineering in general.
>
> (BBC interview 2003)

Side lever engine.
Reproduced by kind
permission of the Scottish
Maritime Museum.

The Clydeside marine engineering works also pioneered the 'side lever', the 'compound' and the 'triple expansion' engines. The efficiency of the triple expansion engines could be said to have opened up the world to the steamship. These engines were developed by Elder and Kirk, both Napier employees. It was Robert Napier himself who developed the side lever engine by moving the beam to the lower part of the engine, making it more stable at sea. Such improvements allowed steamships to travel with a degree of regularity and reliability, putting the old-style wind and weather dependency behind them and operating for first time to a detailed timetable.

These improvements saw a series of important customers, such as Samuel Cunard, who would normally have had their ships built on the Thames, turn to the Clyde (see Chapter 4, p. 112). The Cunard contract spanned 130 years, starting with four relatively small vessels for the transatlantic mail routes and ending with the *Queen Elizabeth II*. The Clyde suddenly had new status. Graham Kennison explains:

> The Clyde was always battling against the reputation of London and was often seen as the 'country' shipbuilding centre. But, now that they were running these crack vessels on a crack route, it really gave them a very, very high profile. So, suddenly, from being the country cousins, they actually became the developers of cutting-edge technology.

The year that Napier and Cunard agreed to build ships for the transatlantic mail run, 1839, was also the year that William Hall designed the *Scottish Maid*. Scotland's contribution to building the great ships was established in that first *annus mirabilis*. From then on, the Clyde dominated marine engineering and shipbuilding. Just before the start of the First World War, there were forty shipyards on the Clyde, which together were building a quarter of all the tonnage in the world. Another *annus mirabilis* occurred in 1913, when the Clyde launched more than 365 ships – a ship for every day.

But even in the heady, successful days before the First World War, when the great liners such as the *Mauretania*, *Aquitania* and *Lusitania* were being built, the Clydeside shipbuilders could have been storing up trouble, sowing the seeds of a crisis for the future. This only really manifested itself half a century later in a programme of closures as the yards found themselves unable to compete with foreign shipbuilders – the result, it is widely held, of consistent lack of investment in the yards.

Robert Napier was desperate for his sons to follow him into the business, but when he tried to retire in the 1850s and 1860s he found the yard could not continue without him. It had been a highly personal project. This problem continued into the middle of the twentieth century. Says Graham Kennison:

> The Clyde in the post-war period was still dominated by a number of family businesses, and it's quite possible that this was one reason for the demise of the Upper Clyde. The families held on too long and tried to keep the power and decision-making in their own hands.

The decline in Clyde shipbuilding can be traced throughout the twentieth century. The First World War was followed by the Depression; and, although the yards were not in good condition, all the stops were pulled out for the Second World War. A period of dramatic growth in the post-war years was fed by a tremendous demand for ships to replace the millions of tons of vessels lost in action. Contracts were plentiful. However, this situation disguised the dereliction of the yards. There was no incentive to modernise; a reinvestment programme would have disrupted production. Short-termism ruled the day.

Elsewhere, in war-ravaged Japan and Europe, the shipbuilding industries were effectively reconstructing themselves almost from scratch. It was difficult for the run-down British shipbuilding yards to compete for state-of-the-art ship orders with these revitalised players. The decline continued through the 1950s and 1960s, the yards struggling on in the shadow of under-investment.

There are now only three shipbuilding yards on the River Clyde. Ferguson's on the lower reaches of the river is the only surviving commercial yard and specialises in smaller but technically sophisticated vessels such as survey ships and oil support vessels. The other two yards on the Upper Clyde – the former Fairfield's and the former Yarrow's – are both naval yards run by BAE Systems, building advanced vessels.

The Hagan boys – shipbuilders

Three generations of Port Glasgow's Hagan family – grandfather Patrick, father Hugo and son Hugh – have collectively 103 years' service in the Clydeside shipbuilding industry, a record that is difficult to match. They agree that, for many years, shipbuilding was at the heart of the town, critical to the well-being

The Hagans – three generations of shipbuilders.

of the community; and, when the industry – in the words of the youngest Hagan – 'went down the pan' in the 1980s, many of the ancillary and service industries that depended on the shipyards were also lost.

The horn that called the men to work and sent them home was a distinctive feature of the shipyard worker's life – and of the community. Grandfather Patrick remembers that it sounded at 7.15 a.m., then 7.30 a.m. and finally at 7.45 a.m., and everyone had to be on their way to work before the second horn went. In the evening, the knocking-off horn was the signal for the men to start setting aside their tools and putting things by, hanging up their old working jackets and preparing for the off, crowding up to the nearest gate until the second horn sounded signalling the opening of the gates. Hugo Hagan remembers: 'They were like greyhounds, you know, bang and away they went. You had to be careful in case you fell, or they'd just run over the top of you.'

As the yard emptied, the traffic outside came to a halt as thousands of men spilled on to the main road outside Scott's or the Kingston yards. A significant number of the men headed for local pubs on a Friday night, and the Hagans remember how the pub managers would have trays of cheap red wine – usually Eldorado – set up on the bar ready for the thirsty shipbuilders.

For Patrick Hagan, ship repair was his preference rather than shipbuilding, and he spent thirty-four years in that line of work. His first job after leaving school at the age of fourteen was an eight-month stint in a shipbreaking yard before he started in the Clyde Shipbuilding Yard as an apprentice shipwright. In 1932, he finished his time, eventually emerging as a carpenter and moving into ship repair. Patrick recalls the harsh conditions:

In the shipyards, the conditions were bad. No cover of any kind. If we were framing or beaming a boat, you were up there on the staging at quarter to eight in the morning and you were there to half-past five – hail, rain, sleet and snow. You simply had to cope with the cold. There were that many people idle at that time – in the '30s. If you didn't do the work, you would be out on the street and somebody else would do it for you. You went out in the morning, got soaked to the skin, came in at dinner time, got stripped right to the skin, right to the nude, everything off, put a new set of clothes on and out you went – two hours later you were soaked to the skin again.

(BBC interview 2003)

Patrick's house in Montgomery Street, Port Glasgow, was a small flat with outside toilets. Six of a family, plus grandmother and grandfather, all lived in a room and kitchen. Cramped conditions meant that it was, in Patrick's words, 'head to tail in the beds' at that time.

In those days, blowlamps were commonly used on the iron bed frames to kill bugs that set up home there, and red lead 'borrowed' from the yard was used to paint these frames, and occasionally the walls, to keep the bugs at bay. To help supplement the family budget, women often went to work in local mills. Gourock Ropeworks, for example, employed a substantial female labour force. However, getting married meant redundancy, and so many married women would take casual work on local farms, picking potatoes and the like.

Hugh Hagan points out that places like Greenock and Port Glasgow were never associated with agriculture but were seen purely as industrial and urban. But, in the 1930s Depression, farmers outside Port Glasgow, in Bridge of Weir and Kilmacolm, would come down in their vans to the tenement streets, and crowds of women would be waiting to be taken to work in the fields. When lay-offs were commonplace in the yards, women would take on the farm work more frequently. The wage was perhaps three or five shillings daily, but they might get a few potatoes home with them … a bonus in such hard times.

Hugh Hagan was made redundant in 1984 as the shipyards began to close down. Even when he left school and started his apprenticeship in 1975, in the same yard as his grandfather, there was still an understanding, an expectation indeed, that a Port Glasgow boy would go to work in the shipyards. Within six or seven years, he recalls, that expectation had evaporated. The security that had been there on and off for two centuries was gone forever.

Patrick remembers 'speaking' for his grandson and helping to get him a 'start' in Lamont's shipyard. This involved approaching the yard manager and asking him if he would give a job to your son or grandson. The Hagans believe that such approaches must have happened thousands of times, building a tradition, a sense of community, pride and continuity both in the shipyards and in the town. Says Hugh Hagan:

> I was quite proud to be sort of stepping into the boots that my grand-father had worn and going into the same shipyard, to be walking down the same road every morning, listening to the same horns. I don't know if everybody felt that, but I was interested in history and I did feel a sense of pride. It was all very sad when it came to an end, you know, because we all kind of expected it to go on. There was great camaraderie, although it was still a dangerous place in my day and everyone had to depend on each other.
>
> (BBC interview 2003)

Patrick Hagan recalls how, in the 1930s and 1940s, the trades – for example, the riveters – were like a family. The rivet team consisted of two men on either side, a 'right-hander' and a 'left-hander', to hammer the rivet into place; the 'holder', who kept the rivet in place from behind the plate; a 'rivet boy' (who could be sixty-five years of age!) who brought the rivets; and a 'putter-in' who passed the rivets to the 'holder'. Uncles and cousins and brothers often worked in squads. The workers were not paid individually; but the so-called 'right-hander', the squad leader, used to collect the money on a Friday night and divide up the earnings between the others, often in the pub after work. This was clearly a dangerous practice, and half a week's wages might be blown in a single night on the bevvy.

Bards of the bilges

One hidden talent which Clyde shipbuilders exported was poetry. Deep in the metal heart of the ships which were destined for service around the world, the workers would scrawl poetry, often in the style of William McGonagall, on the bulkheads. They produced, according to Hugh Hagan, some 'half-decent' stuff. 'I thought that was a great image, this thing taking off to some other country with Clydeside poetry inside it.'

The yards were a bedlam of noise, and the Hagans remember that a shipyard sign language had developed over the years. Hugo recalls one particular day when he was laid off: he had gone over the hills for a walk and could still hear the riveting from miles away.

Bonuses were infrequent; but, at a launch, the team of carpenters who worked to ensure that the ship slid smoothly into the Clyde was awarded a 'bounty' – perhaps £5 in Patrick's day, as much as £100 in Hugh Hagan's time. This led to a post-launch celebration in the local pub.

Launches normally went off without a hitch. Just occasionally, however, there were problems. With a smile, Hugo remembers a launch that was cancelled because of bad weather; but, when the men returned the following morning, they found the ship out on a sandbank. Impatient to get away, she had launched herself!

The appropriately named 'double bottom' in a ship was one of the difficult locations in which the riveters (and, later, welders) had to work – a cramped, enclosed, smelly, dark and dangerous environment, under what was called the tank top. Eventually, extractors were fitted in manholes to extract foul air. Sometimes – even in relatively recent times – the men crawled around working by the light of candles.

Most of all, the Hagan men remember the cold. On particularly miserable days, they would climb an upright every ten minutes to see the hands on the town clock moving slowly and painfully towards 'skailing' (finishing) time. Hugh recalls:

> For the guys working at the stern of the ship down near the river during the winter, it would be absolutely Baltic. They'd get a forty-five-gallon drum and blow a lot of holes in it and burn old wood and stuff. Everybody would gather there for ten or fifteen minutes, get a heat, then take off and do a bit more work, come back and get another heat.

Management did not take kindly to these unofficial breaks and would come along and topple the brazier, say the Hagan men. These severe working conditions undoubtedly took a toll on the health of the shipyard workers in the long term. Hugo Hagan outlines the sort of problems the men faced:

> There were obviously regrets, because most people who worked in the shipyards finished up ill in one way or another. If, like myself, you went in there as a welder, the shell and the bulkheads were all

wet with condensation. And you worked in there all day and you were lying up against the metal; you were frozen stiff. Then in the summertime it was the opposite: too hot, the sweat running from your brow, and you worked in that all day. Conditions definitely went for your health.

(BBC interview 2003)

The Hagans look back with mixed emotions to the end of the era when the Clyde was a major shipbuilding river. There is sadness at the loss of an industry, but the memories of the primitive working conditions are with them still. They all agree that the loss of the shipyards has been a severe blow to Port Glasgow, and they blame the run-down appearance of the district on the lack of money since the closures. All three men paid tribute to the women of the town and the way in which, in hard times, they were always there when needed.

Sammy Barr – electric welder

Sammy Barr, who worked for almost half a century in the Glasgow shipyards before retiring in 1993, comes from a Glasgow family steeped in the tradition. His brother and his father had also been employed in the yards. Leaving school at fourteen, he thought of nothing else but getting into the industry. He got a start with Charles Connell's at Scotstoun. He was happy with the job, probably because he knew almost everyone in the yard, having been to school with many of the younger men.

Sammy Barr.

After two years, he started his apprenticeship as an electric welder, having decided that riveting had probably had its day. The work was easier for smaller men like Sammy in the confined spaces deep in the bowels of the ship. At the other extreme, Sammy would be in the welding shed or on high gantries, wooden staging erected along the hull of the ship. Surprisingly, despite the heights, Sammy thought it was a very safe job thanks to the stager who built the gantries, working side by side with the welders, platers, caulkers and riveters.

In the 1940s and 1950s, safety regulations were something for the future, says Sammy, and the men looked after each other. As there were no showers in the yards, they would arrive home covered in dirt. The first task before tea was to wash off the day's grime.

Sammy returned to the yards in 1954, after two years' national service, to find that conditions had improved markedly with 'real toilets' and changing rooms, and with welding having superseded riveting as he had anticipated. The days of grabbing a sandwich in a filthy corner and trying to get a can of hot water for a brew-up were over – Connell's yard had a canteen.

Sammy always saw welding as a 'quiet' job, compared with noisy work going on around him. Inside his helmet, he admits, he was a bit of a dreamer, recalling the previous night out and other good times, lifting the helmet only occasionally to chat briefly to the man working next to him. Because there was much climbing in and out of the ship, Sammy always felt relatively fit.

It is also the little things he remembers – for example, his toolbox. Sammy had to beg and borrow tools to make up his first toolbox, and once again his national-service years proved to be a watershed. By 1954, toolboxes were supplied by the company. Today, Sammy misses the camaraderie, the way people kept a watchful eye out for each other as they worked, the dinnertime blether in the canteen, the clocking in.

He recalls the solidarity of the Upper Clyde Shipbuilders (UCS) era in the early 1970s, when the workers took over the yards in an historic endeavour to try to preserve the industry and were joined on their vast protest marches by school teachers and children. As a member of the UCS shop stewards' co-ordinating committee during the Clydeside work-in, Sammy was a familiar face to the world's media in the early 1970s. He even travelled to Leningrad in the Soviet Union and to Romania, Bulgaria and Poland to address workers and canvass support. Sammy also figured in talks at Downing Street with Conservative prime minister Ted Heath. He remembers:

> We were known as the Red Clydesiders, which was correct because quite a number of the young lads were Communists. But over

above that I remember the morale being marvellous. Everyone in Britain – in Manchester, London, Liverpool, Newcastle – knew of our struggle and was offering support. I never thought of my personal involvement in all these events. It was about kids coming out of school and finding jobs in the shipbuilding industry.

(BBC interview 2003)

Sammy believes that the Conservative government's decision to increase redundancy payments to £22,000 undermined the fight to retain a substantial, viable shipbuilding industry. He says:

Young people were buying their houses, and £22,000 was a helluva lot of money at that time. I didn't blame them. I didn't fall out with them. It just left us weaker in the fight to keep the yards open. Now we've only two shipyards in Glasgow, Yarrow's and Govan, but I would dispute that we lost the fight. We have won, if only because we still have two shipyards in the upper reaches of the Clyde.

Clydebank – portrait of a shipyard town

Before 1871, the site of the town of Clydebank, on the north side of the river on the western outskirts of Glasgow, was farmland. In medieval times, the monks of Paisley Abbey would ford the shallow river to graze their cattle on the lush meadows at the Barns of Clyde.

The owners of Clyde Bank shipyard at Govan, James and George Thomson, were forced to move by a decision to construct a new dock. They chose a site opposite the mouth of the River Cart – a far-sighted move, as the extra width of the river allowed the launching in the years to come of some of the largest and most impressive ships the world has seen.

The Thomsons retained the 'Clyde Bank' name; and, although workers were at first brought downriver from the city by steamer, tenements were soon springing up along the line of what are now the Glasgow and Dumbarton Roads. By 1882, the Singer sewing-machine factory, one of the largest in the world in its day, was rising below Kilbowie Hill. In 1886, when the population had passed the 5,000 mark, the townsfolk opted for the official name of 'Clydebank'. Rapid population increase was reported in the following decades; and, by the time John Brown & Co., Sheffield steelmakers, took over the yard in 1899, the Clydebank identity had been moulded.

The Provost of West Dunbartonshire, Alistair Macdonald, says the fact that the town was built around the shipyard, rather than the other way round, indicates the part played by shipbuilding in shaping the community. Indeed, the first school, the first bank and the first church were all within the shipyard gates.

Provost Macdonald came to Dumbarton from the Western Isles as a boy, joined the police force and arrived in Clydebank in 1960. He was immediately aware of how important shipbuilding and engineering were to the town. Shipbuilding, in those days, involved a multitude of trades from skilled craftsman to labourer; and, in conjunction with the sewing-machine factory, which at one time employed 16,000 people, it offered work to people of all levels of ability. Says Provost Macdonald:

> There was an opportunity for almost anyone to get a job. It wasn't unknown for someone to start one week in one factory and move the following week to another job. Sadly, that sort of flexibility doesn't exist today.
>
> (BBC interview 2003)

Bobby Dickie is a 'Bankie' – a citizen of Clydebank – and he remembers that, as a boy, the choice for most youngsters in the town was to work either in the shipyards or in the giant Singer sewing-machine factory. He chose John Brown's shipyard because he wanted to serve his apprenticeship as a joiner, giving him a trade he could use in the outside world, just in case he did not enjoy the shipyard work. Says Bobby: 'That didn't happen – I mean, I stayed there for forty-eight years, so I must have enjoyed it!'

One of Bobby's principal memories of the yards is of the comradeship and the characters. He believes the camaraderie was similar to that formerly found across Britain's coalfields – solidarity of purpose and class. He recalls the pride and sense of achievement everyone felt in the ship as it grew through their labours on the slipway. And there was swelling pride tinged with sadness on launch day, when the ship took to the water to leave the yard forever, also signalling probable redundancies among the workforce.

In Bobby's early days, in John Brown's, five or six ships could have been under construction at any one time, with another three or four in the fitting-out basin. The river was booming at that time. In addition to the shipyards, Bobby points out, Glasgow was still a great port, and ships regularly came and went.

Bobby Dickie remembers the events of 1971, with the announcement that Upper Clyde Shipbuilders was to go into liquidation, and the effect that it had on the town.

Deserted shipyard.

When the news broke, it was a shock – a tremendous shock to the people of Clydebank, because the yard had been there for a century and more. It was part of a tradition. It was the finest shipbuilding yard in the world – at least as far we were concerned. People could just not believe it. Personally, I felt really shattered. It wasn't just the shipyard that was closing; it was all the subsidiary companies, the local firms, who supplied materials. It was a sort of domino effect. If the yard closed, all these other industries would suffer.

(BBC interview 2003)

The famous work-in gave some respite, and the former John Brown's shipyard became an oil-industry construction site; but Clydebank today looks back on two decades that have seen the community lose not only the shipyard but also the Singer factory. It is a much-changed place. Says Bobby Dickie:

It is sad when you pass the yard now: there's nothing left. The skyline at Brown's has changed – only one crane left. The other sad thing is that with the number of people who worked in the yard the community was alive, the shops and obviously the pubs were busy … that has all changed, there's nothing of that left. Where Singer's was is now a business park, but it doesn't employ nearly as many. There was always something going on in the shipyards; it was on the newsreels and helped give Clydebank its identity. To a great extent that has now been lost, the character of the community has gone. But other industries are coming, not employing the same number of people, but hopefully Clydebank will be here for a long time to come.

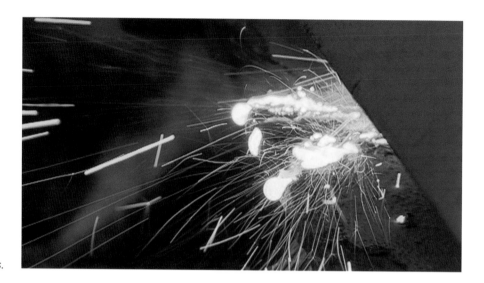

Welding sparks.

Provost Macdonald believes that people the world over were touched by the plight of the Clyde shipyards:

> The name John Brown's echoed round the world. It was recognised all over as a symbol of the best possible in shipbuilding and engineering. And there was further sympathy because of the Blitz which devastated the town in 1941, hundreds killed and hardly a house left undamaged. The spirit of the people was such that they said: 'Right, we'll just get on with it.' I've always thought the phoenix was an appropriate symbol for Clydebank to adopt. From a very small spark which one could hardly detect in times of peace

Dismantling the shipyards.

and prosperity, when things got tough, that burst into a flame of resistance and determination that, no matter what happened, we were not going to allow it to beat us.

Provost Macdonald sees diversity as the keynote for the town's future prosperity. The days when the local economy was based on one or two large industries, he believes, are gone forever, and the closure of one of these new businesses could never have the same devastating effect.

The Provost is also anxious that there might be children leaving school today who have little or no knowledge of the town's remarkable industrial history. Every ship that left the Clyde was recognised as being the best in the world, and every ship that left John Brown's was recognised as being the best on the Clyde, according to Provost Macdonald. He has a dream that one day a museum will be created in the town – perhaps on the site of the shipyard – which would identify the thousands of artefacts which the town still possesses associated with shipbuilding and engineering:

> I have a vision that people will come from all over the world and stand on the shipyard grounds, saying: 'My God, I'm on the holy ground. I'm actually standing where my grandfather, my father and generations of our family worked.' The museum would remind people of our wonderful historical and industrial past. That said, we have to look to the future; but anyone who doesn't learn from the lessons of the past is foolish. Perhaps, someday, Clydebank will be famed for something other than shipbuilding. However, we must accept that, for the town, the noise and bustle of the shipyard is gone forever.

The UCS work-in – making industrial history

The decline on the Upper Clyde, which led to the great changes in Clydebank and along the river generally, was already becoming apparent by the mid-1960s. The Geddes committee, established in 1965 to investigate the British shipbuilding industry with a view to making it internationally competitive, recommended the amalgamation of the five yards – Fairfield's, Ferguson's and Stephen's of Govan, Connell's and John Brown's – which resulted in the creation of Upper Clyde Shipbuilders. The Conservatives came into power, and one of their policies was not to support what they described as 'lame ducks'. In 1971, UCS had a cash-flow problem and were looking for the government to lend them £6m. To no-one's surprise, the government refused.

In June 1971, as people were about to go away on their annual holidays, there was an announcement in the House of Commons by John Davies, the Secretary of State for Trade and Industry, that no money would be forthcoming and that a liquidator was to be appointed. The proposal would have meant that UCS, which employed some 8,000 people, would shed almost half the jobs. For people who had been in shipbuilding all their days, this was a real tragedy. There would be no retraining, no second chance.

Over thirty years on, Jimmy Reid, the workers' leader who became a household name in the subsequent campaign, has no doubt about what should have happened decades before:

> The British government should have recognised the historic contribution that shipbuilding in general, not just on the Clyde, had made during the wars and, indeed, during peace. What was needed was an investment programme that should have made our technology away at the cutting edge, and we should have taken on more sophisticated vessels and left some of the vast hulks that were being built at that time to others in the Third World.

Archie Gilchrist, managing director of Govan Shipbuilders from 1972–4, offers a different perspective:

> The Clyde shipyards had worked extremely hard all through the war to turn out as many ships as possible regardless of cost, but as quickly as possible, with the result that a lot of the equipment was pretty clapped out. The Germans, on the other hand, had most of their shipyards flattened by British bombs and were helped by aid after the war to rebuild their shipyards – in some cases on greenfield sites. So they, then, had a very considerable competitive advantage over the under-invested British yards who had been working their socks off during the war and hadn't had the time or money to spare for re-equipment.
>
> (BBC interview 2003)

However, 1971 was a watershed, a moment of history for the shipyard workers of Clydeside. They opened the famous gates of the John Brown's yard at Clydebank, invited the world's press inside and announced that they were in charge and that they were about to become involved in an international campaign for the right to work.

Initially, there had been a mood of pessimism about how successful any industrial action might be; but, after several meetings of the shop stewards' committee, the decision had been taken to organise the work-in. This was new territory, but the workers' leaders had felt that there was no point going on strike or staging a sit-in. As Bobby Dickie says:

> Once the idea took hold, tremendous support was forthcoming from local people, from the workers and their families and from local churches. To be masters of our own destiny was something new, and it was something that at times we felt a wee bit apprehensive about. It was something that had never been tried before, anywhere. But, as the campaign continued, we felt more confident that at the end of the day we would have a victory. I think we were fortunate on the Clyde that we had excellent leaders: Jimmy Reid, Jimmy Airlie, a whole number of people.

Backing, both financial and moral, flooded in from all over the world – from places as geographically and politically far apart as the Soviet Union and the United States of America – for this unique campaign, and there were major demonstrations in both Glasgow and London. The workers and supporters were kept informed almost hourly on everything that was happening. Bobby Dickie looks back to that support and the growing feeling that there was 'no way' the UCS workers could or would let their supporters down, no way that they could fail. Money for the fighting fund poured in, the workers each contributed 50p weekly from their pockets, and fund-raising concerts were held.

The work-in ended in September 1972, with Govan and Connell's being saved, and an American oil company, Marathon, of Texas, taking over the John Brown's yard in Clydebank. The irony of the situation at Upper Clyde Shipbuilders was that, immediately before the liquidation announcement, there was no problem with the productivity of the yards, which, in fact, was increasing. There was work – something like thirteen or fourteen ships on the order books – but there was also a cash-flow problem. However, there was a legacy of massive under-investment in the yards. A glut of shipbuilding after the Second World War was not balanced by reinvestment. When Wayne Harbin, president of Marathon, came to look over the Clydebank yard, he was astounded that the *QEII* had been built there with the resources that the yard had at that particular time.

Archie Gilchrist.

Jimmy Reid, for one, believes that Britain has never cherished the skills of the shipbuilders. He remembers a series of dredgers being built at Govan for the Soviet Union, and meeting a Soviet official who suggested that Britain must be 'dripping with talent' because these were the best dredgers he had ever seen – and yet the capacity for building them was being closed down. 'Your country must be so abundant in talent you can just scatter it to the winds.'

Archie Gilchrist points out that the decline of shipbuilding was not confined to Scotland:

> When I was working on the Clyde, the shipyards in Sweden were held up as being the absolute example of the most efficient shipyards in the whole of Europe; they are nearly all closed down now. So it's not just the Clyde, or Britain, it's really the whole of Europe. Because shipbuilding is capital-intensive, you need money. But you also need cheap labour, and, of course, you don't get that in Europe now.

While war-damaged yards in Europe were rebuilt from scratch, and the Japanese and Americans got themselves organised, the yards on Clydeside were trying in the 1950s and 1960s to compete using the same old pre-war equipment, working in an outmoded shipbuilding environment. 'We were using tools that looked like they belonged to Fred Flintstone', says Jimmy Reid.

Archie Gilchrist agrees:

It is quite difficult to understand how they could make ships with such dilapidated equipment, but of course they had served apprenticeships and were most of them extremely skilful.

In 1971, payments, which every yard gets at various stages in the construction of a ship, were, according to Jimmy Reid, withheld. 'It was,' he says, 'a manufactured liquidation … it need not have happened.'

Jimmy Reid – a yard full of memories

Jimmy Reid remembers the noise and the clamour of the busy workplace:

> The noise inside the yards was diabolical. First time I ever went into
> a yard as a boy, I thought I was in hell. It was deafening. You were
> holding your ears. That's why a lot of the old guys were deaf.

Shipbuilding was always a dangerous industry, ranking alongside fishing and mining for accident risk, and Jimmy Reid believes that this bred a kind of natural solidarity in the yards, each worker depending on the other for his safety. Like Clydebank, Govan, where Jimmy Reid lived, was very much a shipyard community:

> You had this marvellous relationship between the community and
> the workplace. On occasions when a real problem arose, perhaps

Jimmy Reid.

with landlords in the community, the workers in the yards would use their industrial power to supplement action, for example by the womenfolk over rent. What you had was a culture which sprang from the industry by which the men earned their living.

Reid believes that, more than in any other industry, shipyard workers identified with the product of their labours. One reason was that mass production was impossible – a production line of Cunarders would have been unthinkable. The work progressed slowly, and there were stages without any appreciable difference in the ship; but work went on internally. Like an organic process, the ship grows. The launch saw this identification with the product; this love of the beautiful object, which they had built, laid bare: 'It's leaving the river, and I've seen men upset. It's like a daughter that you love leaving home, and you worry about what will happen to her.'

This view is shared by Archie Gilchrist, among others:

> Shipbuilders would bring their families in to watch a launch because they had been working on a particular ship for perhaps two or three years. When they saw it floating away, they thought: 'well, that's something: there's a bit of me in that ship'.

Jimmy Reid regards the UCS workers' action as a victory, as evidenced by the yards that still remain on the Upper Clyde. More than that, he believes that shipbuilding need not have contracted in the way that it did:

> People say it was outmoded, an old technology. Nonsense. There is no real alternative to the most economic bulk transportation of goods throughout the world – by ship. Our shipbuilding industry wasn't destined to die – because ships are still being built – it's just that we're not building them.

CHAPTER 3

Harvesting the Oceans

When people talk about Scotland's offshore resources, thoughts tend to turn to the North Sea oil industry, the nation's biggest economic mainstay of the second half of the twentieth century. However, since earliest times, Scotland's most fundamental ocean resource has been fish. The fact that the fishing industry, at the start of the twenty-first century, is facing the greatest crisis in its history is all the more poignant when you consider the extent to which it has been an essential part of the nation's fabric. For centuries, while Scotland sustained a relatively poor and underdeveloped economy, this abundant source of nutritious food was too accessible to be ignored.

The 'silver darlings', from the film Drifters, *by John Grierson. Film Images, Crown Copyright.*

One fount of fishing knowledge in nineteenth-century Britain, a gentleman called James Bertram, declared that, given its size and its relatively small population, Scotland has been as active as any of the larger nations in exploiting the fish stocks around the coast. From Lerwick to Eyemouth, from Aberdeen to Campbeltown, indeed all around the Scottish coast, towns and villages developed which, to a great extent, owed their existence to the riches found in the sea. Archaeological evidence shows that the earliest known residents of Scotland, the hunter-gatherers, had a very substantial fish diet. And the diet of early peoples was to modern eyes reasonably exotic. The 5,000-year-old kitchen midden of the oldest standing house in north-west Europe, at the Knap of Howar on Papa Westray, Orkney, is crammed with oyster shells. Whale vertebrae from a later period suggest that whale-hunting was not unusual (see Chapter 1).

We also know that herring have been fished in an organised fashion for many hundreds of years. In 1666, it was reported that unusually plentiful catches in the River Forth were causing anxiety in many Scots. It was whispered that such a herring harvest could only be an omen of some misfortune to come. From the previous century, there are reports of great foreign fleets fishing off the east coast.

Categories of seafood taken from Scottish waters have changed very little over the millennia. Four principal groups can be identified. Starting on the seabed, there are the crustaceans. The Papa Westray oysters, as well as mussels, lobsters, crabs and other exotica such as 'spoots', or razor fish, fall into this class. The next group are the bottom-dwelling fish which marine scientists classify as 'demersal' – these are the familiar white fish such as cod and haddock as well as the less frequently enjoyed saithe, plaice and sole. Above them in the water column are the pelagic fish – the herring and the mackerel. Bridging the world of the sea and river are the fourth category – salmon and sea trout – fish that spend part of their adult lives in the ocean, travelling astonishing distances to spawn in Scottish rivers. In the medieval period, it was herring and salmon that formed the bulk of Scotland's fish catch and exports.

The high price of fish

The United Kingdom has kept statistics about injury and death in the workplace for well over a century, and fishing has the unenviable honour of topping that league table for most of the period. It is generally accepted as one of the most hazardous callings and was particularly dangerous in the days when sailing vessels were the primary components of the fleet. Records suggest that a major fishing disaster tended to come along every ten to fifteen years and, every year without fail, there was a drain on the fishing fleet – and the communities that supplied crew members – through losses at sea.

A quick trawl through the files of *The Scotsman* or *The Herald* reveals how the spectre of death at sea has hung constantly over the fishing communities of Scotland right up to the present day. The cruel ocean is not discriminating and has regularly taken the crews of foreign vessels as well as home-based boats.

1885   Five men were drowned when an unnamed Campbeltown fishing boat capsized shortly after leaving harbour.

1911   Four fishermen were drowned when the Carradale skiff *Mhairi* was struck by a squall and sank in the Kilbrennan Sound between Arran and Kintyre.

1928   Eight crewmen were drowned when a trawler ran on to rocks on the Orkney island of Hoy.

1933   The Granton trawler *Succession* sank in the North Sea after a collision with a Liverpool steamer; eight fishermen were drowned.

1933   The Aberdeen trawler *Venetia* was wrecked after running aground three miles north of Stonehaven; the crew of nine were drowned.

1953   The eight-man crew of a Milford Haven trawler were lost when she struck rocks off Coll in the Hebrides.

1959   The fishery cruiser *Freya* sank off Rattray Head in Caithness with the loss of three lives.

1959   The trawler *George Robb* was lost near John o' Groats with her crew of twelve; thirty-four Aberdeenshire children were left fatherless.

1972   The Fraserburgh seine netter *Nautilus* was lost in the North Sea with her crew of seven.

1978   Hope was abandoned for the Fraserburgh fishing boat *Enterprise* and her eight-man crew missing in the North Sea.

1980   The Buckie trawler *Bounteous* sank with the loss of three of her six-man crew.

1980   Three fishermen were drowned when a seine netter sank in a storm after colliding with the Aberdeen harbour breakwater.

1986   Eighteen seamen were drowned when a French trawler sank west of the Hebrides.

1997   Four fishermen were drowned when the *Sapphire* sank twenty
        miles off Peterhead.

2000   Seven men were drowned off the Isle of Man when the *Solway
        Harvester* sank in a severe storm.

According to Dr Robert Prescott, the director of the former Institute of
Maritime Studies at St Andrews, one particular storm in the mid-1800s was a
catalyst in attempting to improve the conditions under which Scottish fishermen
worked and to increase their chances of surviving the frequent gales which batter
the nation's coast. He explains:

> There was a particularly bad gale in 1848, a summer gale off the east
> coast of Scotland, when a very large number of boats were caught
> out at sea at low tide and were unable to make harbour. At the time,
> most Scottish harbours were tidal and in poor condition. It was
> impossible to enter them except for a few hours on either side of
> high water. This disaster, in which over 100 boats and their crews
> were lost, was so appalling that Parliament set up a Commission
> of Inquiry under Captain Washington, and he toured Scottish
> harbours interviewing fishermen and boat-builders about the
> causes of the disaster.

Wrecks strewn across the bed of the North Sea are testimony to the hard-won
nature of the skills involved in harvesting the ocean. The *Budding Rose* is such
a vessel. Around 100 miles out of her home port of Peterhead in 1988, she filled

with water and sank. All of the crew were rescued by an RAF Sea King helicopter. Other fishermen over the years have not been so fortunate.

Peter Bruce was skipper of the *Budding Rose* and is now in command of the latest vessel to carry that promising – even optimistic – name. He fishes pair-seine – two boats with one net astern, attached to both. A trawl can last for four hours. On a good day, the catch can be five or six tons of fish, mostly cod or haddock. The haddock goes to Scotland, cod to England and monkfish to France and Spain. The fishing community, and skippers like Peter, are facing economic catastrophe as well as the constant threat of disaster at sea.

The skipper's story

The **Budding Rose** I work is the third one in this family. It was built in 1990 in Campbeltown. My father had the first boat built in Aberdeen in 1974. Then my brother and I bought the Peterhead-built **Budding Rose** which sank. I suppose it might have been a frightening experience, but I didn't really think about it. I had responsibility for the whole crew, and if anything had happened to them I don't think I could have lived with myself. With hindsight it probably was traumatic, but it was worse for my wife. On the day that the boat went down, we'd just moved into a new house and she got a call saying the boat was in trouble and they were trying to rescue me. Fishing is still important in our family, although I'm the only one working in the industry. My great-grandfather was a fisherman, so was my grandfather, my father, myself and my twin brother. My son is thirteen now, but I don't think I want him to go into the fishing. The life is too unpredictable, precarious. No, it's not the life I want for him. It's very depressing now – every month more families leave the fishing – families that have even more history and heritage than we do. Before, you knew heaps of guys who were fishermen, but now you meet people in the street and they ask: 'Are you still at the fishing?' I can see my kids having to move away because there'll be nothing for them here. If you listen to the scientists, you'd believe there were no fish left in the sea. That's just not my experience. Fish stocks generally maybe aren't as good as they were in the '80s and '90s, but haddock stocks appear to be as good as they have been in the past thirty years. Even the scientists agree with that. Peterhead's getting really sad; it's losing its identity because it's losing its fishing. A few years ago, 120 boats were decommissioned all at once. That was terrible for Peterhead. This time, there are sixty-nine boats being given the option to decommission. Even if they don't want to, banks are putting the pressure on — if payments on boats aren't kept up, they have no choice. Some of these boats are only three years old. I still get a lot of satisfaction when I bring in a good catch, but it's a very depressing time for the industry.

Chasing the silver darlings

Scotland's bountiful fishing grounds, the finest in Europe according to most authorities, were by the 1400s attracting huge fleets of vessels from the Low Countries and the Baltic, hundreds strong. This huge surge in activity followed the development of a technique whereby oily species of fish were cured with salt in barrels. In the early Middle Ages, most Scottish herring was caught in the inshore waters of the Firths of Forth and Clyde.

The Dutch operations were much more highly organised and subsidised than the long-established fishing activities around the Scottish coast. The continental fishing was conducted using large, seagoing herring busses – substantial ships that could spend long periods at sea, carried many acres of nets and cured the fish on board. Each buss had several smaller boats in tow to carry out the catching. Working on the principle of safety in numbers, they arrived 'mob-handed' in the Scottish North Sea, or the German Ocean as it was then styled – great armadas of busses that, from time to time, were protected by warships. They operated near the Scottish coast, particularly around Shetland.

During their summer feeding and spawning migration, the main stock of herring came from their wintering grounds near the Norwegian coast to the coast of Scotland. The wide migratory sweep took them close by the Northern Isles before continuing down the east coast of Scotland. In principle at least, the Scots should have been better placed to exploit the shoals using smaller boats and shore-based curing.

Scottish kings and governments looked with dismay at the foreign fleets plundering what they saw as a national resource. James VI, first monarch of a United Kingdom of England and Scotland, had, like rulers of a sovereign Scotland before him, tried to ensure that foreign fleets, the great armadas of boats from the Low Countries and the Baltic, should recognise the exclusive rights of Scottish fishermen to their own inshore waters.

In 1594, James VI granted the Dutch a licence that permitted them extended fishing privileges in Scottish waters. According to one unauthenticated tradition, during the reign of James V, a number of Dutch fishing busses had breached the licence that permitted them extended privileges within Scottish waters. The king, incensed by the outrage, promptly sent a barrel full of pickled Dutch fishermen's heads, their names written on cards and attached to their foreheads. It was clear, though, that there was very little that could be done. It would have been impossible for Scotland with its pocket-size navy to police the fishing grounds. Issuing proclamations and cutting off the occasional piratical head was, in fact, ineffective. The answer had to be found in the economic field. The Scots saw the need to increase the size and scale of the home-based effort, but it was not until the late 1700s that the main stimulus for expansion came with the introduction of bounties. Initially these bounties were for building boats, but later they were more successful, when payments related to the quantity of herring landed. As Dr Prescott explains, the government was later to introduce an innovative quality-control method:

> The Crown Brand, as it was called, was only applied to herring of a particular quality which had been cured in a particular manner using high-quality products, good-quality salt and barrels. This Crown Brand scheme later was so effective that it actually removed continental opposition to a great extent.

Herring is a particularly nutritious fish, but only if it is cured very quickly after being caught. One of the Crown Brand criteria was that the herring had to be packed in salt within twenty-four hours of being brought from the sea. These dramatic developments in Scotland's herring fishery soon saw Scottish-cured

The Crown Brand.
Angus Council,
Cultural Services.

herring being sold all over Europe, particularly in Catholic countries where the 'only fish on Friday' church ordinance saw a huge demand for pickled herring.

In addition, the British Empire opened new opportunities, and in the 1700s Scottish fishermen – from both the Firth of Clyde and the east coast – were helping to supply the plantations in the Caribbean where cured fish was the diet of the slaves, and were also helping to meet a demand for fish in North America.

In 1809, the Fishery Board was established with offices set up along the coast. Officials were appointed to inspect the cure, ensuring that the herring were

Herring tales

Throughout the development of the herring fishery, the value of nets was regularly above that of the boats! Early nets were hand-made from linen or hemp, but from the 1820s bigger factory-made nets came in. The changeover to cotton nets from the 1860s resulted in lighter nets which in turn allowed the boats to carry more. This meant that, when the boat was lying with its nets 'shot', they extended about two miles from the boat.

Herring tales

The process of inspection to achieve the Crown Brand involved having sample barrels opened top or bottom, at random. From each barrel, the fishery officer would select a pickled herring and take a bite out of its back. Brightness of scales, firmness and flavour all influenced his decision. If awarded, the brand signified that the herring would keep in any climate for twelve months.

properly gutted and sorted. They inspected the barrels and put the distinctive Crown Brand on those barrels containing high-quality fish. By the 1860s, Peterhead and Fraserburgh on Scotland's north-east shoulder were rivals of the great northern herring station at Wick. The season could be extended by going further afield. At the other end of the map, Shetland became important as an early summer fishery. Another telling factor in the expansion of the herring industry is that from 1870 boats ventured further out to sea. Where the fishery had once been concentrated within ten or fifteen miles of the coast, it now extended to up to fifty miles or more.

The introduction of bigger steam-powered vessels in the second half of the nineteenth century increased pressure on herring stocks. That pressure was

Branded herring barrel, Signal Tower Museum, Arbroath. Angus Council, Cultural Services.

unrelenting and continued right through to the third quarter of the twentieth century. First of all the steam drifter, a very powerful fish-catching machine, was introduced, and then a whole new generation of motor fishing vessels appeared which were better able to exploit the fish stocks. They could operate more independently of wind and tide and in weather and sea states that might have forced sailing vessels to abandon fishing.

The net result was that herring stocks – unpredictable at the best of times – began to decline. The fish had always been truly fickle, coming and going from the fishing grounds in a manner that no one had been able to understand – or predict. This brought lean years among the boom years of the nineteenth century. Other factors also came into play: the advent of seine netters brought an end to the old-style herring-fishing. During the First World War, fishing was an even more dangerous business than usual, and a large number of vessels were taken up for Admiralty service as supply ships or for minesweeping duties. At the end of the war, fish stocks had recovered to a certain extent, but the market for herring never regained its pre-war buoyancy. There was distress in the industry; and economic and political problems in Germany and Russia, the main consumers, in the years before the Second World War, added to the crisis. Several countries – notably Norway, Iceland and Germany herself – were challenging the great lead that Britain had built in the herring trade. At home, white fish such as cod and haddock became the fashionable taste, normally accompanied by chips. The result was twenty years of painful contraction and readjustment for the herring industry in Scotland.

At its peak, the Scottish herring fishery had been an impressive operation. On the eve of the First World War, the main Scottish drifter fleet comprised 1,000 boats, and, in the early years of the twentieth century, the Scottish herring cure could reach over two million barrels – several times the maximum achieved by the Dutch.

It had taken all of four centuries to achieve, but Scotland did lead the way in the exploitation of one of its own greatest natural resources – the silver darlings. Today, the three dozen Scottish herring boats using modern methods have as much catching power as the much larger fleets of earlier times; and, although they still catch herring, which are limited by quota, their main fishery is now mackerel. Also, with the great conservation difficulties facing the white-fish fleet, the pelagic-fish sector of mackerel and herring is now the most popular and secure in the Scottish fleet.

Herring bones

1138 David I, of Scotland, granted the Abbey of Holyrood the right to fish for herring on the Firth of Clyde, one example of a number of such charters granted to religious houses.

1303 The official measurement of herring, a *last*, was fixed as 100 *long hundreds*, and a *long hundred* as 120 herring.

1493 Continental fleets were active in Scottish waters; James IV urged all maritime burghs to build twenty-ton vessels and to be zealous at the fishing, and pressed idle persons into that service.

1542 A plan to colonise the Western Isles with Fife fisherfolk finally collapsed.

1609 James VI forbade foreigners from fishing off the Scottish coast without a licence.

1718 Fishermen were rewarded by a bounty scheme both for landing fish and for the building of boats; the fishing season was regulated and regulations continued for over a century.

1727 Creation of the Fishery Board for Scotland.

1786 The founding of the British Society to Extend the Fisheries and Improve the Sea Coast of the Kingdom; the aim was to build fishing villages to relieve poverty.

1815 Scottish Fisheries Act. All nets set or hung within two leagues of the coast on a Sunday were forfeited.

1860 After driftermen complained about ring netting in Loch Fyne, an act prohibiting the catching of herring on the west coast was implemented during first six months of the year.

1868 Registration of fishing boats became compulsory: each boat had to display its identifying code on both sails and hull.

1880 Mission to Deep Sea Fishermen founded: they sent boats with tobacco and medical help to Scottish boats combating Dutch and German 'gin' boats.

1889 The quarter-cran basket was legalised as a unit of measurement for herring in Scotland.

1900 A fishing laboratory, which was opened in Dunbar in 1893, shifted to Torry in Aberdeen; it also controlled the administration of fishing around the Scottish coast and operated several research vessels.

Pulteneytown

So quickly did the herring industry around the Scottish coast grow that the catching operations quickly outstripped the available onshore resources – harbours, accommodation for the itinerant herring-gutters, and storage facilities. Thomas Telford, the Langholm civil engineer, was called in to build herring ports capable of handling the burgeoning industry.

Although the cumbersomely titled *British Society to Extend the Fisheries and Improve the Sea Coast of the Kingdom*, founded in 1786 under the presidency of the Duke of Argyll, bought land at Tobermory, Ullapool and Caithness for redevelopment, the most famous project of these by far is Pulteneytown, a 'suburb' to the south of Wick in Caithness. This purpose-built fisher community has its own harbour capable of providing sanctuary for hundreds of fishing vessels, not just locally owned boats but also seasonal visitors.

Pulteneytown, Wick.

Telford was sent by the Society in 1792 to Wick, to a location which, because of its expanse of level ground, the convenient supply of water and the abundance of building stone from five local quarries, was attractive for their ambitious scheme. The existing community of Oldwick consisted of only ten inhabited houses, and it was decided to name the 'new town' after William Johnstone Pulteney, the governor of the Society.

Approval was given in 1801 for the development, and work started in 1803. The comprehensive plan included housing, a new harbour and facilities for all the ancillary industries such as sail-making, barrel-making and curing. This local production kept much of the prosperity within the community, and the

William Johnstone Pulteney, later 5th Baronet, c. 1772 (oil on canvas), by Thomas Gainsborough (1727–88). © York Centre for British Art/www.bridgeman.co.uk

scale of the operation is reflected in the fact that four sawmills worked day and night to produce 250,000 barrels annually.

The story of Pulteneytown is not one of unbridled success. Recession, the Napoleonic Wars and the unpredictability of the herring shoals led to a slow start. The fishing, when it did get under way, was of course seasonal as the herring moved up and down the Scottish coast. Hard months came with the winter: two poor seasons at the fishing were enough to impoverish a family. Eventually, with people flocking to Wick from many places including the Hebrides – walking across Scotland looking for work – there was inevitable overcrowding, poor sanitation and outbreaks of cholera and dysentery. The population of 6,000 more than doubled when the migrant workers arrived.

A sense of community was built, however, with the pubs and churches as the focal points. Drink became a problem. Because of the very unpleasant damp and cold conditions at sea, men would often take whisky with them as a comfort and to warm them on a cold night. Herring-curers sometimes sealed a deal to land fish with a bottle of whisky for each man on the boat. Whisky was flowing through the industry. It became a cause of social distress, and the attempts to control its use became the stuff of legend. The Duke of Sutherland even offered free coffee to men who promised to remain teetotal while at sea. The temperance movement set up rooms – usually converted shops – to provide non-alcoholic alternatives to the public houses.

It took twenty years to establish fully all the partner industries in Pulteneytown. By 1822, there was a resident population of 3,000. This huge influx of people was generated not only by the herring boom but also by the contemporaneous Highland Clearances. According to local Wick historian Ian Sutherland, the promise of some kind of employment in the booming herring trade brought many people who had been put off their land. Most of the seasonal workers who came to Wick/Pulteneytown lived in dormitories above the yards or in attics. Only a few lucky souls found comfortable lodgings. Sanders McNab grew up in Pulteneytown and started at the fishing himself in 1972. He recalls with affection growing up in Telford's town:

The Pulteneytownman's story

My mother was a gutter and my father was a buyer. When I was growing up, Pulteneytown was a hive of activity with every entry and building being used by people working in the herring. There was a strong sense of community, and when we were kids we were forever running in and out of each other's houses. No-one minded. You just had to get on with people – everyone was there to work and we were pretty poor, not dirt-poor, but hard-working. If everyone in your street is poor, you don't get discontented. I lived in Upper Pulteneytown. Lower Pulteneytown was more or less a rabbit warren with lots of people put up in very small houses. When we were young, I hardly ever remember going across to Wick. Pulteneytown was our whole world. For children, there was always plenty to do – fishing, rock-climbing, all kinds of mischief. My mother was a gutter, and ninety per cent of the kids at school had mothers in the gutting, so when school was finished we'd run over to the yards because everyone's mother was there. They worked from 5 a.m. to 10 p.m. most days – no one would do it now. In the season, the place was so busy. Every available space had someone living in it. There was no friendlier place. We never locked our doors – everyone trusted each other – but on the other hand, I suppose, we had nothing worth stealing! I still go down to the harbour every morning, and I remember when it was so busy. Now there are less and less boats all the time. You aren't even allowed to land herring here any more – it's not a herring designated port.

(BBC interview 2003)

The development of Wick's 'wee sister' was no short-term improvement programme. Expansion was a consistent factor in the story of Pulteneytown over a century and more. The harbour grew on the basis of Telford's plans until 1900, and the town was completed by 1911. The infrastructure was too small to house everyone who wanted to live there, however, and the harbour – originally designed for 300 boats – was also badly stretched. Pulteneytown was a victim of its own success.

The design of Pulteneytown was revolutionary – in the same mode as the stylish parts of Edinburgh and Bath – but with an industrial purpose. The industrial heartland was in Lower Pulteneytown, on ground reclaimed from the

> The rapid expansion is reflected in the fact that, in 1783, Wick had produced 500 barrels of herring, and by 1815 the annual figure had soared to 50,000 barrels.

Herring-curing yard, Shaltigoe, Pulteneytown. From the Johnston Collection, in the custody of the Wick Society, at the Wick Heritage Museum.

river. This was where the curing and gutting took place. Upper Pulteneytown, by contrast, was the residential area. The further back from the river you lived, the higher your status.

Older people in the community remember the lilting Gaelic spoken along the quays and the stench from the curing yards that crowded the shore. George More was born in Pulteneytown in 1924:

> There was an awful stink from the gutting factories, but in this part of the world there was usually plenty of fresh air to blow it away. The wind could be bad; there were days when you weren't allowed outside for fear of blowing away. It was only on the still, quiet days

that it really did pong. But we knew just to get to the windward side
of it and we would be okay.

(BBC interview 2003)

When the season finished in the north, the boats went to Yarmouth and
Lowestoft. The gutters and the coopers, the crews and the drifters – perhaps
as many as 6,000 people – would suddenly vanish, and the place became like
a ghost town.

Most of the Telford houses are still intact, and the Wick Project has recently
been given a lottery grant to refurbish some of the old properties with a view
to turning them into flats. The Heritage Centre, in Pulteneytown's Bank Row,
is packed with thousands of fascinating photographs, reconstructions and
memorabilia of the days when herring was king.

Come a' ye fisher lassies

The herring boom brought about some remarkable changes for women in
Scotland. In an era when suffragettes were struggling to assert their rights,
thousands of Scotswomen and girls travelled independently across the country
to work at the fish-gutting in ports like Wick. They often followed the fishing
south as far as Lowestoft or Yarmouth or even Ireland. Herring-processing was
a very labour-intensive business, much more so than the white-fish industries.
Speed is critical in ensuring that the fish are quickly cured.

Operating at tremendous speed, and with remarkable dexterity, women
exclusively provided the labour for this gutting, salting and packing. Some of
the most skilled gutters, knife blade flashing, could process up to fifty-eight fish
per minute. Usually, the gutters were either young girls or old women, those
who could most easily get away from home.

In the Highlands, in particular, this migrant army, who would return home
at the end of the season, put a brake on emigration and changed the shape of
the economy. More importantly the 'fisher lassies', who learned their trade from
their mothers or aunties, were an independent, mobile workforce. This was at
a time when men did no household chores and most women were anchored to
the drudgery of the kitchen sink and what we might call 'homemaking'. These
pioneers travelled across the country, living in strange places with lots of young
men around, away from parental control and influence. Most historians of the
fishing industry agree that the experience, while testing, was a positive one for
most of the women, giving them a world view and a feeling of self-confidence

Herring gutters, Wick. From the Johnston Collection, in the custody of the Wick Society, at the Wick Heritage Museum.

seldom found in their peers. They were, in a very modern sense, liberated. Their work and, of course, their income constituted a significant element in the domestic economy. It was one way in which younger women stacked up money to get married. Often, fishermen would come ashore at a distant port to find their womenfolk, wives and daughters, sisters and nieces, all fisher lassies, in town for the gutting.

It is difficult to imagine nowadays how hard and dirty the work expected of the gutting crews could be, standing for long hours in the open air at the fish trough, hands bandaged to prevent gashes and sores, damaged fingers being constantly immersed in brine. The salt, if it found a cut, would simply eat into the hand. Women usually worked in threes, two of them gutting and one, normally the one with the longest arms, as the packer. Their gear included rubber boats and an oilskin apron with bib and obligatory headsquare. Rita McNab, of Lerwick in Shetland, is now seventy and started gutting when she was just fourteen. She confirms the positive side of the experience:

The herring girl's story

I was fifteen and I wanted to travel. My mother wouldn't let me, so I went behind her back and signed up with the Glasgow girls. It was my way of getting a working holiday.

They gave you what they called arles, and you signed a paper saying you wouldn't work for any other firm, then you just made for the train station and followed the crowd. You landed up at the Isle of Man, you had to find your own accommodation, and you started from there.

The cooper came and said to me 'Have you done this before?' and I said 'Aye', but I hadn't. I'd never seen a herring, let alone worked with it! So I started to pack my barrel, but I did it upside down. Herring should be packed bellies up, but I packed backs up, and the cooper said 'How long have you been doing this?' 'Two years', I said. 'I think there's a wee lie there!' he said. 'Let's try bellies up.' And that was my training. You had to keep up with the gutters or there would be trouble. You had to get as much herring in your barrel as possible, because that's what made the money, not the wages – I think it was £1 or £2 a week – and you'd to pay your digs and everything out of that.

I started at Isle of Man, then Lerwick was always a holiday camp. You had your own hut – three girls to a hut – and you done your

Rita McNab, former herring girl.

hut up something unreal, fishboxes draped with cloths, a jar of dandelions for your flowers – but you never spent anything, just what you could find or the local folk gave you.

Yarmouth was cold and sometimes you actually had to break the ice on the top of the barrels. There were no rubber gloves. We learned to protect our hands with clouts, we made up batches from linen and you wrapped every finger individually. In the morning, the cooper would come and roar 'Come on and get yer clouties on, lassies, there's a lot of herring at the pier', and you knew you were going to have a busy day.

The worst problem was if you got a fish scale in your eye. It seemed to vacuum onto your eyeball, and it was really sore and could mean going to hospital. It happened to me one particular time and it was the cooper, an elderly man, he got me up against the wall and waited till I opened my eye and took me by surprise and he just licked it out with his tongue. The tongue is rough and it seems to move the scale for some reason. I often wonder if doctors would do that today!

When you got home at night, there was no such thing as a bath or shower, so you washed the 'three F's' as the saying goes. You scrubbed yourself till you shone, and then you went out to meet a'body. I don't think anyone who's been there regretted it. It was a good life. It wasn't much money but you were free. I wouldn't have missed it for anything. I call it my National Service!

(BBC interview 2003)

It is essential at this stage to draw a distinction between the fisher lassies and the fishwives. Ironically, while their 'sisters' were asserting themselves in the shoreside curing yards, the fishwives were possibly among the most put-upon of women. They were women, often in the smaller fishing communities,

---

Herring tales

The best-known fisher clothes were unquestionably those worn by the fishwives of Newhaven on the Forth. They rose to prominence after being spotted by Queen Victoria on her first visit to Edinburgh. The fishwives, particularly at Musselburgh, also had a reputation as fine footballers and athletes!

who held the fort while their menfolk were at sea. On top of their customary household chores, they were totally involved in the work of their husbands, mending nets, collecting bait and fixing the bait to the line (some lines had as many 1,000 hooks).

Other tasks of the fishwife were to prepare the fish for sale and to hawk the catch round the neighbourhood. When the men set sail from villages where boats were simply hauled up the shingle and refloated, the women would howk up their skirts and 'float' or carry their men on their backs through the surf to the boat so that the fishermen's long boots, softened with sperm oil, remained dry for the voyage. Ballast was an essential for every voyage, and the fishwives would regularly carry enormous burdens of stones in baskets to the boats. As one North-East fishwife declared: 'We'd a' tae work like slaves, nicht and day'.

Boats of all shapes and sizes

Scotland's fishing fleet has shrunk dramatically in recent years, and to a certain extent the vessels that are left – whether they are the multi-million-pound white-fish boats with their own cinema for the crew, or more modest two-man creel boats – have become standardised within their own sectors. However, in the nineteenth century and in the first half of the twentieth century, each fishing coast of Scotland had its own particular designs for its boats, customising them to local needs. These designs were a matter of much local pride. Examples of the boats that have been rescued and renovated by enthusiasts are to be found up and down the country.

Throughout the period, there was always a marked difference between east-coast and west-coast boats. The fishing boats in the Clyde estuary and the Western Isles spent most of their time working in relatively sheltered waters, but they had to be nippy in order to negotiate shoals, sea lochs and strong tides. The line-fishing boats on the Ayrshire coast were open sailing boats, between twenty-four and twenty-eight feet long, and were called 'nabbies'. Bigger boats, over thirty feet long, then appeared, with a small fore deck for a crew of three or four men. The straight-stern boats, of which there were a number of local variations, were called 'skiffs' and were used for line and drift-net fishing.

The Northern Isles of Orkney and Shetland developed a style of boat that was used principally in their own waters. The boats were pointed at both bow and stern – popularly known as double-ended – and raked fore and aft. This

Reaper, a 'fifie' herring drifter built in 1901 and restored at Anstruther.

reflected the long historical connections in the islands with the Norsemen and their master mariners, the Vikings. Many boats were indeed imported in kit form from Norway, as a result of the shortage of timber in Orkney and Shetland. The main variations were the sixern, the fourern and the yole, the design of each being more or less identical but with variations in size. The sixern, which, as the name suggests, is powered by six oars and is the largest of the group, was quite capable of venturing many miles out into the open North Sea or the Atlantic. The Yole was a much smaller boat, approximately nineteen feet long with a beam of about nine feet, with plenty of storage space for nets and ropes and ideal for inshore fishing among the voes and skerries. Its flexible, light build made it adept at riding the waves and bending with the forces of the water. Its simple rigging and square sail took great skill to operate.

Compared with their west-coast counterparts, east-coast boats were altogether more rugged as they faced up to the unpredictable open waters of the North Sea. From Wick to the southern shores of the Moray Firth, the 'scaffie' was favoured. These boats measured twenty to forty feet in length and had a curved stem and forefoot and a sharply raked stern. This made the keel relatively short and allowed the boats to turn easily. Normally they were rigged with one or two masts, even three on the largest vessels, with lug sails.

Coull Deas, retired fisherman, now volunteer crew member of the Reaper.

They were very light so that they could be beached easily by their five-man crew. They had a surprisingly large working space for their size but lacked the ability to run with the wind that was characteristic of the more heavily built 'fifie'. The fifie was most commonly used from Aberdeen southwards as far as Eyemouth. The stem and stern were almost vertical, and the tendency was to build them bigger than the scaffies, measuring up to sixty-five feet or more. They had a long straight keel, and this made them fast, but not as manoeuvrable as the scaffie. The fifies had two masts and used a simple rig with an unstayed foremast, but it still required great skill to use safely. Crewmen risked being swept overboard when the sail was swung round as the boat tacked. In Shetland, the smack rig was preferred as it was easier to handle in

restricted waters where frequent turning was required. The lug sail had to be lowered and raised on the other side of the mast every time the boat tacked.

It is interesting to note that neither scaffies nor fifies were decked until 1885. The common belief was that open boats were safer and easier to work. However, it was due to the persistence and example of the Royal National Lifeboat Institution, who built a partly decked boat and showed that it worked well, that fishermen were eventually persuaded to convert to boats that were decked and safer in heavy weather.

The Zulu type of fishing boat was introduced by William Campbell of Lossiemouth in 1879 with his vessel *Nonesuch*, and was an attempt to combine the best features of both the fifie and the scaffie. It featured a vertical stem and raked stern. The Zulu, so-called because the Zulu wars were raging in South Africa at the time of its development, was an immediate success and quickly came to dominate the east-coast fleet. There was continual fine-tuning of the design: steering wheels replaced the traditional tillers around 1895, and steam-powered capstans were introduced in the 1880s. The latter took over from hand-powered winches, allowing a greater weight of sail to be handled, and so led to the building of bigger boats.

At their peak, Zulus were an impressive eighty feet in length. The mast was as tall as the keel was long, and the boat was crewed by seven or eight men and a boy. Commercially, it was a fast design, giving a speedy return to port with catches that exceeded the capacities of both the fifie and the scaffie.

The other 'Battle of the Atlantic'

The first serious skirmish over cod between the UK and Iceland was in 1958 when the UK tried to prevent Iceland from extending her fishing limits from four to twelve miles off her coast. The second dispute was in 1972–3, when Iceland extended her limits to fifty miles; but it was the so-called 'cod war' of the mid-1970s that was the most highly charged.

Between November 1975 and June 1976, the UK and Iceland faced up to each other over Iceland's decision to proclaim her authority over the ocean up to 200 miles from her coast, including bountiful fishing grounds that had traditionally attracted fishing boats of a dozen nationalities. Iceland feared that these other countries were depleting and over-exploiting the fish stocks that were estimated to have been reduced by a third in the 1970s. The Icelandic government and fishing authorities pointed out just how dependent their economy was on fish. On average, these catches represented ninety per cent of the country's total exports, and it was felt that the time for drastic action had arrived.

The UK refused to recognise the 200-mile limit and continued to fish within the disputed area. Iceland deployed eight ships – six coastguard vessels and two Polish-built stern trawlers converted into coastguard ships – to enforce her control over fishing rights. In response, Britain deployed a total of twenty-two frigates. Normally between six and nine were on station at any one time. Seven supply ships, nine tugboats and three auxiliary ships to protect Britain's forty fishing trawlers joined the armada.

The situation deteriorated, and reports came of British trawlers having their nets cut by the Icelandic coastguard and of numerous rammings between Icelandic ships and British trawlers or frigates.

Captain Kettlewell's tale

We were sent there with other ships to protect the fishing, which is a lot more difficult than it sounds. The only way to do it was to get between the fishing boats and the Icelandic gunboats who were armed with large cutting mechanisms. They would literally come at any time from their harbour; they had radar and aircraft that could plot where the trawler fleets were. So they could be guided and then attempt to go straight for them and cut the warps. Our role was to make it quite clear to the Icelandic gunboats if we could that we weren't going to have any of this nonsense. We set out with a very robust rule of engagement to drive them off. It was

Captain Nick Kettlewell,
RN Commander,
HMS Brighton, *1975.*

possible, particularly at night, to shine searchlights on their bridge and blind them. We had large tugs there ... who endeavoured to ease them off by altering course by small amounts; if they were outside us we could ease them off the trawlers, but then they were more manoeuvrable than us. Once they learned that trick they could dodge under our stern. When that happened, the trawlers had to really bring their gear in. The gunboat could ram the ships at some speed – it could rip open a section of the hull say ten, twenty feet long. This could let in an enormous quantity of water and divide the ship up. They never rammed me because I don't think they ever wondered what I was going to do to them if they did. It really was a matter for political negotiation and not the Navy trying to fight off gunboats and it cost us a lot and we didn't get any more fish in the end either.

(BBC interview 2003)

The 'war' caused Iceland to threaten to close the NATO base at Keflavik, which in turn would have had serious repercussions on NATO's ability to defend the Atlantic Ocean from Soviet incursions. With mediation by the Secretary General of NATO, Dr Joseph Luns, Iceland and the UK were able to come to an agreement on 2 June 1976. This deal set a limit of twenty-four British trawlers within the 200-mile zone at any one time, and four conservation areas were closed permanently to all British fishing. In addition, Icelandic patrol vessels were allowed to halt and inspect British trawlers suspected of violating the agreement. This lasted only six months, after which British boats were excluded permanently.

Many fishermen read this agreement as capitulation by the British government. Compensation claims for losses suffered as a result of the cod war are still being pursued and settled. In one compensation payout, fishermen and former fishermen in Aberdeen, which had twenty-one trawlers involved in Icelandic waters, received 252 payments amounting to £1.3m. John Gowie was a fisherman during the cod war:

John's tale

We had no other option because in our opinion the Icelanders were taking unilateral action with no legal support so we thought, well, we'll just carry on fishing until they *do* get legal support. It was our job. We had no other option. We couldn't do anything else. It was our chosen profession so we pursued it with all the enthusiasm and energy we could muster. There was an urgency and impetus from the Icelanders that we hadn't seen before. The atmosphere was always very tense as you never really knew what was going to happen. It was quite dangerous. If the ships were rammed in a vulnerable spot – near the stern, for example – they could have been sunk. They introduced these wire cutters for cutting the trawl wires that were connected to the trawl on the seabed. If they cut those wires then that was you. Thousands of pounds worth of fishing equipment lying on the seabed. It meant you had to stop fishing. The time wasted replacing the lost gear was phenomenal. It's not a viable proposition to not be fishing and be watching someone else's gear. Fishing is a business and you have to be catching fish to make money. In 1976, when they finally succeeded in acquiring their 200-mile exclusive zone, then we had nowhere to go. For every fisherman there are five or six shore workers dependent on them. The butcher, the baker and the candlestick maker all depend on the fishing.

(BBC interview 2003)

All for the nation's fish and chips

Fishing for cod, haddock and whiting was a long-established industry round Scotland's coast, but in the twentieth century it was to gain a position of prominence. For example, there was an important 'hook and line' cod fishery

in Shetland in the eighteenth and nineteenth centuries. However, as the herring stocks were seen to decline around the North Sea in the mid-twentieth century, and as there was a marked reduction in the market for cured herring, Scotland's fishermen had to look for alternatives. From the 1960s, white fish were the main take in Scotland.

The growth of the urban, industrial centres and the collapse of the herring-fishing led to greater exposure of white fish in the markets. The haddock in particular became a very popular catch in Scotland.

Because demersal or white fish hug the seabed, the types of vessels and equipment had to change from smaller fishing boats with nets to larger trawlers that raked the bottom of the sea pulling in everything in their path – a technique that has been consistently criticised for damaging marine wildlife. Scots fishermen have always been near- or mid-water operators. Large vessels, which formed part of the distant-water fleets from the likes of Grimsby and Hull, were of little use, such was the proximity of the Scottish fleet sailing from Granton, Peterhead and Aberdeen to large, local fishing grounds.

White fish were landed predominantly at Aberdeen during the 1950s and 1960s; but, as the emphasis in Aberdeen switched to oil, and the fishing industry in the Granite City was plagued by labour disputes in the 1970s, Peterhead gradually established itself as the largest white-fish port in Europe.

Handling the white fish in bulk caused new problems for the fishing industry infrastructure.

White fish, being a fresh product, are not cured by pickling in brine. They have to be shipped away quickly, so the need for a good transport network to underpin the industry is obvious. Fishing harbours with good transport links – such as Peterhead, which faces some of the best North Sea grounds and with connections to the hungry industrial centres – came into their own. Further-flung centres such as Wick or the island fishing ports just could not compete.

The fear today among conservationists is that the cod may have been over-fished like the herring before it and is now threatened with extinction in the southern parts of the North Sea. Such a scenario has already unfolded in Newfoundland, where the cod-fishing has been closed for a decade.

Contraction of the Scottish fishing industry experienced in the twentieth century is clearly reflected in the statistics. In 1938, over 17,000 fishermen in 5,000 boats made their living from the sea; but, by 1970, the number of fishermen employed had dropped to 9,000 and the number of boats almost halved. Most recent figures – for 2002 – are even more alarming. It is calculated that Scotland's fish-catching sector lost one in seven of its workforce through continuing contraction. The number of working fishermen fell from 6,637 to 5,707. With up to 100 white-fish boats decommissioned in 2003, the picture is bleak. In addition, for every catching job lost, it is estimated that up to half-a-dozen ancillary jobs disappear. The devastating effect on the fishing communities is obvious.

The fishermen, who feel let down by both the Scottish and the European governments, believe that if tie-up and decommissioning continues at the rate it has done in the past decade, then the cod fleet will disappear within five years.

CHAPTER 4

The People's Ocean

The voyage of the *Hector*

Although the Scottish connection with the sea is an ancient one, ocean voyaging was beyond the experience of the vast majority of ordinary Scots until the middle years of the eighteenth century. Fishing brought most Scots into regular contact with the sea, but this was mainly around Scottish coastal waters. There were, however, in the late seventeenth century, a few bold buccaneers in the ranks. For example, hundreds were caught up in the Darien fiasco, an abortive attempt to establish a Scottish colony in Central America between 1695 and 1700.

Those who made long sea journeys were most often military adventurers, colonial officials, religious fugitives seeking sanctuary, or prisoners-of-war. Covenanters, who were fugitives from religious persecution, were transported during the troubles of the mid-seventeenth century. Into the eighteenth century, Scottish doctors, lawyers, factors, foremen and overseers joined them to form this preliminary, small-scale emigration. The Caribbean was the most common destination in the earliest phase. Professional seamen returned to Scotland with tales of faraway places with strange-sounding names; but, for most Scots up to the mid-eighteenth century, the prospect of venturing beyond the confines of their market town or clachan was a daunting one. It was said that, in this period, if an Orcadian was required to take sea passage to London, he was advised to make his will before he left. The thought of crossing the Atlantic must have been terrifying.

West India Docks.
© Guildhall Library,
Corporation of London/
www.bridgeman.co.uk

In the period before the great economic upheavals of the Napoleonic Wars and the widespread enforced Clearances, emigration was already seen as the only escape to genuine independence and a better life. People with a little money were preparing to take a chance, tear themselves away from their ancestral lands and head off for the promise of better things in the New World. By 1800, it is thought that as many as 150,000 Scots had emigrated to North America.

Dr Marjory Harper of the University of Aberdeen, Scotland's foremost emigration expert, describes this development:

> This was a fusion of grievances, discontentment with things going wrong at home and attractions that were leading people overseas. People were discontented with restricted horizons in terms of renting farms or acquiring extra land, or indeed acquiring jobs … but they were increasingly aware of opportunities on the other side of the Atlantic, particularly in terms of owning their own land rather than simply renting it.

(BBC interview 2003)

The prospect of owning a parcel of their own land without having to answer to a landlord motivated these eighteenth-century emigrants to make the most gruelling of sea voyages. They were the first of over two million Scots who emigrated before the First World War, principally to Canada, the United States, Australia and New Zealand. Every single journey to the new life required an often harsh and always dangerous sea voyage halfway across the world. Many tens of thousands succumbed to the rigours of the journey.

Dr David Dobson of the University of Aberdeen Research Institute of Irish and Scottish Studies is in no doubt about the momentous nature of the emigration decision:

> For the majority, it truly was a leap in the dark. Many people had never been on board a ship in their lives, perhaps had never even seen a ship if they came from some inland parish. The truth is that they didn't have a great deal of choice. The Highlanders had to move south to the growing industrial towns or go abroad if they wanted to maintain their communities, their language, perhaps even their religion.
>
> (BBC interview 2003)

Emigration became increasingly commercialised during the course of the eighteenth century and into the nineteenth century. It was a phenomenon that was regularly aired in the press. It was also a topic of daily conversation across the land as more and more people knew someone who had taken ship for 'America', which, until the American War of Independence in the 1770s, described the entire North American continent.

Replica of the Hector.

Where it all started at the head of Loch Broom.

In 1773, the *Hector*, a three-masted former Dutch barque, was the first ship to bring emigrants directly from the Scottish Highlands to Nova Scotia. Those 189 passengers were among the vanguard of a great army of emigrants to the Canadian Maritime Provinces and to the great forests and prairies of Canada over the next 200 years, and their story is held up as an example of Scottish resilience and determination.

The pioneers on the *Hector* were victims of a scam. Two entrepreneurs had bought land in the Pictou district that was intended for these Scottish immigrants; but, by the time they arrived, the prime shorefront land had been sold on, and the *Hector* passengers had to settle for inferior plots. The Scots complained, and troops were even called from Halifax to quell any threat of civil disorder.

Loch Broom.

The people who travelled on the *Hector* had been tenant farmers in the north-west Highlands and Islands who had struggled to survive the post-Culloden chaos when all the old clan values were turned on their head. They had been recruited for the *Hector* with the promise of free passage, a plot of land and provisions to last them through the first year. The records of the voyage show that thirty-three families, twenty-five single men, their agent and the obligatory piper were on board when the *Hector* left Loch Broom on 1 July 1773. The departure took place from a site near the present-day fishing port of Ullapool.

It was 15 September before Nova Scotia was in sight, at the end of a horrendous voyage during which the emigrants were battered by storms and

Launch of the replica of the Hector. © *Wee House Productions, J. Meir/ S. Mackay, Pictou, Nova Scotia.*

blown halfway back to Scotland. As they began to starve, they were reduced to scraping in the bilges for mouldy oatcakes thrown away earlier. The voyage had taken two weeks longer than scheduled. Eighteen children were lost to smallpox or dysentery.

The *Hector* contingent settled quickly on the new land, despite the initial setbacks, and they soon made headway towards prosperity. They pleaded with their remaining friends and relatives in Scotland to join them. By 1803, there were 5,000 people settled in the community of Pictou as the Scottish emigrants continued to spread across the vast acres of Canada.

In September 2000, Nova Scotia Scots, including a contingent of direct descendants of those brave folk from the *Hector*, celebrated their heritage with

Advertisement for a sailing of the Hector, Edinburgh Advertiser, *1773. By courtesy of Edinburgh City Libraries.*

For PICTOU HARBOUR in NOVA SCOTIA. BOSTON, and FALMOUTH in NEW ENGLAND.

THE SHIP HECTOR, JOHN SPEIR master, burthen 200 tons, now lying in the harbour of GREENOCK. For freight or paſſage apply to John Pagan merchant in Glaſgow, Lee, Tucker, and Co. merchants in Greenock ; and in order to accommodate all paſſengers that may offer, the ſhip will wait until the 10th of May next, but will poſitively ſail betwixt and the 15th of that month.

N. B. Pictou harbour lyes directly oppoſite to the iſland of St. John's, at the diſtance of 15 miles only.

the launch of a replica of the ship that carried their forebears to a new life in North America. Some 140,000 Canadians and Americans can trace their ancestry to the passenger list of the vessel. The launch was part of an annual Scottish Festival at Pictou which has featured a re-enactment of the first landing in 1773, pipe bands and other peculiarly Scottish pastimes, workshops on Gaelic, piping and fiddle-playing and a kilted golf tournament.

Our most precious cargoes

Ireland and Norway are thought to top the European table of nations which 'exported' their people, principally to North America, during the great era of emigration between 1815 and 1914. Statistics can disguise more fundamental truths: Scotland was never far behind with the proportion of her sons and daughters who opted or were compelled to emigrate. When you consider that as many as 600,000 Scots may have settled in England during the same period and are not included in the figures because they are classed as internal migrants, then the Scots were, undeniably, among the most numerous emigrants.

The exodus began in the eighteenth century although, generally, at this early stage, landlords and the government greeted the idea with disapproval. Overpopulation was not a word in the dictionary at this period, and the goal was still to retain people as the source of the nation's wealth. From the era of the American Revolution (1776) through to the end of the Napoleonic Wars (1815), emigration eased a little, due to government discouragement and the risks involved in travelling during a climate of war.

Advertisements of the time stress how well equipped boats were – guns fore and aft – in an attempt to attract more customers. In the last years of the eighteenth century, the British government was slightly better disposed to the idea of emigration to Canada, where they realised that a new population might act as a buffer against American expansionism. Mass emigration, however, was still regarded as a threat to national integrity. Dr Harper of the University of Aberdeen explains one of the devious measures employed to hold emigration in check:

> In the period 1803–55, Passenger Acts were passed which improved conditions on board emigrant vessels, such as ensuring that each person had a reasonable living space. On the surface, this sounds very humanitarian; but the first act passed was designed to bring emigration to a halt. By increasing standards, the price of passages

rose; thus it became too expensive to travel. The Highland Society of Scotland was basically the landlord lobby behind it all.

After the Napoleonic Wars ended in 1815, the Scottish economy collapsed into depression. Soldiers returned from continental wars to find a land without work, and widespread poverty. Landlords now began to change their attitude to emigration when it appeared that they might have to foot the bill to feed this growing and increasingly redundant population. Suddenly 'emigrating' their superfluous tenants became an attractive proposition for the landowners, many

Points of departure

West-coast ports were the most important in terms of shipping people to North America. They faced the Atlantic and avoided the hazardous journey through the Pentland Firth which was necessary for journeys from Aberdeen. In the nineteenth century, Greenock, established as a fishing port in the late seventeenth century, increasingly became Scotland's major embarkation point. When steamships began to replace sailing ships, the smaller ports began to fall out of the picture. Previously, small ports up and down the west coast despatched clusters of emigrants. The shipping agents sent their vessels to call in at far-flung locations such as Loch Broom, Loch Hourn or Loch Linnhe to collect their passengers rather than forcing poorer emigrants to travel to the Central Belt. In the nineteenth century, east-coast ports such as Aberdeen, Peterhead, Fraserburgh, Montrose and Cromarty came into the emigration equation. Over 15,500 emigrants left Aberdeen between 1830 and 1872; Banff, a much smaller community, saw 600 emigrants leave. These smaller departure points were most important during the nineteenth and early twentieth centuries when many ships were visiting the Highlands and Islands. Two famous examples of these were the **Metagama** and the **Marloch**. The latter sailed in 1923 from Stornoway with 300 emigrants. Greenock, however, close to the hub of Scotland's growing industrial conurbation, remained by far the most convenient point of departure, and the Tail of the Bank became for many thousands the spot where they left Scotland behind – forever.

of whom were keen to transform their estates into profitable sheep farms. From 1825, they began paying the passages of their tenants. Maclean of Coll, for example, the laird of Rum, funded the emigration of 300 of his 350 islanders to make way for sheep. Many did not want to leave, but they had no real choice – emigrate, or be evicted with nowhere to go.

Some chose to leave on ships that had brought timber to Scotland from Canada; others left on whalers and cargo ships. It was not until 1830 that custom-built emigration ships began to appear. Timber was a bulky but cheap cargo, so the boats needed a cargo to fill the hold on the outward trip – emigrants were a readily available commodity. Aberdeen, for example, had some sixteen agents vying to secure customers on the voyage to Canada. Needless to say, passages arranged by landlords tended to be the cheapest on offer. The journey to Australia and New Zealand was more costly, and the government was still anxious on principle not to fund emigration but, instead, to allow free-market economic forces to dictate appropriate population levels. However, they did assist with bounty schemes funded by the sale of colonial land in Australia and New Zealand. Because these involved government-chartered ships, conditions tended to be better, and mortality rates were lower.

The voyage in the late eighteenth and nineteenth century was tough, hazardous, strange and occasionally terrifying. Dr Harper believes there is always a danger of overstating the horror stories of emigrant voyages:

> It is undoubtedly true that people did die at sea – they died in ship-wrecks, they died when the ship caught fire, they died of epidemic disease – but then many people who stayed at home died in similarly unpleasant ways. It wasn't the emigrant voyage that was particularly to blame for these tragedies, and I think we need to keep some sort of sense of balance here, because most of the people who did embark on an emigrant ship did arrive safely at their destination. Certainly it wasn't usually a pleasant experience, but they did make the journey, they did arrive and they did manage to set themselves up in the new land.

The decision to emigrate was a huge, life-changing moment because, although there is evidence of some return emigration even from the sixteenth and seventeenth centuries, for most it was irreversible. Most people went to the New World and severed ties with everything familiar – family, friends, home ground. The most dramatic impact was felt in the Highland communities where large extended family groups sailed together. People from Lowland Scotland tended to go out more as individuals, as artisans perhaps emigrating under indentures (fixed-term working contracts). Says Marjory Harper:

> It wasn't such a life-altering factor for the communities which they left, because they were going in ones and twos and their departure wasn't noticed in the same way as say, the departure of 300 people from a particular glen in the West Highlands. So the impact would *always* be dramatic on the person who was going and *sometimes* dramatic on the community which they left, but that depended very much on how many people were leaving from that community.

By the mid-nineteenth century, a complex emigration network had developed in Scotland that touched almost everyone in the population in one way or another. Merchants would advertise their ships by a variety of methods: newspapers, handbills, posters in pubs and personal testimonials from previous passengers. Positive letters from relatives who had already made the journey were important in encouraging emigration inquiries. There were professional agents who acted almost like travel agents, some employed by the receiving governments. The arrival of the railways and the use of steam instead of sail for the great voyages made it easier, faster and safer to emigrate.

Greenock and then Port Glasgow became by far the largest of the emigration ports. The exodus simply became part and parcel of daily life in these locations. Mass emigration from Glasgow really started in the 1860s. This was the era of the industrial emigrant. Agents were active in Glasgow using incentives and dubious sales patter to entice people on to boats bound for South Africa, Australia and New Zealand, Canada and the United States. Journeys to North America were always more attractive because they were cheaper and shorter than the voyage to Australasia. Agents would trawl the Highlands and Islands with slideshows, which were still a novelty in those parts, and address communities in churches and village halls.

How steam transformed sea travel

It is perhaps not widely recognised that, as the eminent historian Gordon Donaldson so neatly put it, 'Steam navigation had its birth and infancy in Scottish waters'. It was in the 1780s that Patrick Miller experimented with the first steam-powered vessel on Dalswinton Loch. In 1802, William Symington's experimental paddle steamer *Charlotte Dundas* was charging along the Forth and Clyde Canal at an impressive five miles per hour; and, in 1812, Henry Bell unveiled the *Comet* (see p. xii), the first steam-powered vessel to operate successfully in tidal waters.

The arrival of the steamship was to bring fundamental changes to the lives of people in the Highlands and Islands. In a very real sense, and whether they wanted it or not, these new-fangled steamers brought them into contact with the modern world. From the outset, the steamship left its main competitors – sailing vessels and horse-drawn road transport – in its wake, and it had become well established before the great British steam-railway network reached across the land.

Its advantages over sail among the islands were immediately obvious. The two names most associated with steamship development on the west coast are David Hutcheson, who formed his company in 1851, and David MacBrayne, whose nineteenth-century steamships not only brought Victorian tourists to the Highlands but also made the transportation of every conceivable item from cattle to coal scuttles so much easier. The impact of these companies is perhaps reflected in the maxim that declares: 'God made the world, but David MacBrayne made the Highlands!' On the east coast by 1821, there was a regular service between Leith and Aberdeen followed within a few years by the important Leith-to-London link. The steamers were finding their way to the northern and western isles with regularity; and, on Scotland's inland and sea lochs, they served communities as well as the burgeoning tourist industry. In 1831, the publication of the third edition of a 'steamboat companion' listed almost sixty steamer routes and schedules.

The names of those early steamers – *Iona*, *Columba*, *Royal Scot*, *Glengarry* and *Glencoe* – became household words; and, with coal relatively inexpensive in the first half of the twentieth century, the shipping companies put a great premium on the shovelling capacity of their stokers.

Steamships could complete longer journeys often as quickly as a train. The shipping companies loved to race each other, not just to steal customers on the jetty but also out of the sheer pleasure of 'ruling the waves'. The steamship network spread wider and wider. By the 1830s there was even a St Kilda service, and services to Orkney and Shetland were started around the same time. In the 1880s, a steamer connection was in place to Norway. The length of service of some of these ships was remarkable. The *Earl of Zetland* operated in Shetland waters for nearly seventy years; and an even greater achievement was probably that of the *St Ola*, which plied the turbulent waters of the Pentland Firth between Caithness and Orkney from 1892 to 1950.

Steam, as well as boosting international trade, also altered the shape of Scottish emigration. The number of emigrant ports declined as the focus moved to larger centres such as Glasgow and Greenock. In tandem, the huge technological strides which were being achieved in transport and communication meant that rural populations were not restricted to their regional departure point; they could travel south where they would have a greater choice. Smaller ports were unable to handle the more complex docking procedures of the larger iron-hull steamships. Fares became a third more expensive, but there was no dip in the emigration levels despite the extra expense.

The arrival of steam shipping by the mid-nineteenth century revolutionised sea transport. Ships could travel faster and could guarantee arrival times. Industry on both sides of Atlantic benefited from faster turnover of goods; and, as these great industries flourished, more people were needed to service them. Points of access were opening up all over the New World, in particular at New York. The floodgates of emigration were opening.

In the days of sail there had been different classes of travel, but most travelled by steerage. With the advent of steam, the differences became more obvious with the famous state rooms of the famous Cunard, White Star or P&O liners. The steerage or third-class accommodation in the steamships was a vast improvement on the old sailing ships, but it remained basic dormitory

The saga of No. 534

From the 1920s, Cunard operated its weekly service from Southampton to New York with three ships, the **Aquitania**, **Mauretania** and **Berengaria**. In 1930, the company decided that it wanted two ships to maintain the service, and the era of the 80,000-ton liners was born. The new vessels were to be half as big again as their predecessors. Work began at John Brown's yard at Clydebank on **Hull 534**, the first of the new sisters. The plan was for her to be the biggest, fastest, most luxurious, most talked-about ship in history. But there were problems. The Depression was biting, the bank withdrew overdraft facilities from John Brown's, and it was clear to many that Britain could not sustain two rival companies, Cunard and White Star, on the North Atlantic passenger run.

With **534** over three-quarters complete, work stopped on Hogmanay 1931. For over two years the yard lay silent, the great hull of the liner looming starkly over the town until a merger was forced on the two shipping companies by the government. This saw a promise from Westminster of £9.5m: £3m to complete **534**, £1.5m for working capital and £5m to build the other vessel.

In April 1934, to the skirl of the pipes, the workers streamed back into the yard, and within a few months **534** was set for launching. Everyone in Scotland seemed caught up in a growing frenzy as launch day approached. Hotels, bed-and-breakfasts and boarding houses in Glasgow and surrounding towns were fully booked for the proposed launch date within weeks of the men returning to work – months before the launch. Ship **534** dominated cinema newsreels, newspaper stories and street-corner gossip. For the launch, John Brown's workers were given priority viewing sites – 9,000 of them received tickets to the launch in their pay packets, tickets that placed them near the royal party. More than 30,000 people crammed the empty yard next to Brown's, and 1,000 packed the pleasure boats on the Clyde. Small passenger planes did a roaring trade with commercial flights. The Clydesiders needed no telling that this was an historic event; but, just in case the rest of the nation had not got the message, John Masefield, the Poet Laureate, was commissioned to write a poem.

Clydebank's pride was launched on 26 September 1934 by George V and his wife, Queen Mary. The **Queen Mary**, the favourite liner of everyone from Churchill to Marlene Dietrich, had space for 2,038 passengers and 1,285 officers and crew.

space. A steerage passenger might, on occasion, be elevated for an evening to entertain the toffs; but, in general, mixing was not encouraged.

In the years before 1914, the diesel engine was beginning to make its mark. The golden era of steam in Scottish waters had come and gone, but one splendid survivor of the paddle-steamer era remains: the *Waverley*, which proudly announces herself as 'the last sea-going paddle steamer in the world'. Her story is told in Chapter 6.

Cunard's floating cities

The Clyde's connection with the most famous name in commercial shipping – Cunard – stretches right back to the first years of Queen Victoria's reign when Cunard's wooden paddle steamer *Britannia* took to water for the first time. Only 207 feet in length, and weighing in at a modest 1,154 tons, her maiden voyage on 4 July 1840 from Liverpool to Halifax, Nova Scotia and Boston marked the inauguration of regular steam-driven travel across the Atlantic.

Samuel Cunard, a Canadian from Halifax, came to London in 1839 with the intention of securing the Admiralty tender for the first transatlantic shipping line to carry mail between Britain and America. From the outset, Cunard's intention was for his service to be of the highest quality. Despite warnings from London and Liverpool – suspicious, perhaps even envious, of the rapidly developing Clyde shipbuilding industry – he drew up a contract for four ships to be built on Clydeside with the marine engines constructed by Robert Napier.

Cut-away view of the Queen Mary. See front endpaper for a larger view. Reproduced with kind permission of J. and C. McCutcheon.

Napier, a Victorian industrialist, probably did more than anyone to make the Clyde the world's pre-eminent shipbuilding river. His most significant contribution was unquestionably as an innovator of steam engines. Many of Napier's engineers went on to found shipbuilding companies of their own. Among these were the brothers James and George Thompson, whose company was later to become the John Brown Shipbuilding Company at Clydebank, arguably the world's most famous shipyard and home of the great Cunarder Queens of the twentieth century.

Throughout the 1850s and 1860s, technological improvements continued. Iron replaced wooden hulls, then steel replaced iron; screw propellers replaced paddles. The journey time across the wide Atlantic shrank to eight days. Each successive decade saw liners of greater speed, size and luxury being added to what was largely a 'Clyde-built' fleet. The most famous examples of the Cunarders are *Queen Elizabeth*, *Lusitania*, *Aquitania*, *Queen Elizabeth II* and, of course, the flagship *Queen Mary*.

For more than a century, Cunard helped to underpin the Scottish economy. It is thought, for example, that over 100,000 people were involved in some way in the construction of the *Queen Mary* during the 1930s.

The enthusiast's story

Jeanette McCutcheon is a self-confessed enthusiast. In 1979–80, her parents took her to see the **Queen Mary** at Long Beach, California, where the vessel has been berthed as a floating hotel, conference centre and tourist attraction since being retired in 1967. 'I just fell in love with her – I thought she was the most beautiful thing I'd ever seen. Now I'm one of the biggest collectors of **Queen Mary** memorabilia in the UK.' The Queen made 1,001 voyages, says Jeanette, and was the only liner from her stable to make it into retirement. 'She is still one of the most popular ships afloat, and she was the pinnacle of Scottish engineering. Scotland can be totally proud of her.'

Conflict gave Scots another reason to cross the oceans. During the Second World War, the great liners were requisitioned as troop ships since their vast size made them invaluable for moving huge numbers of men very quickly. One of the stipulations for renewal of the funding to complete the building of the *Queen Mary* had been that this would be part of her role. The liners were stripped of their luxury, painted in camouflage grey and put to work ferrying troops, tanks and supplies. The main rule that the Admiralty laid down was 'No stopping – for anything', and they zigzagged their way across the oceans to avoid submarines.

Passenger capacities for all the liners were increased dramatically: the *Queen Mary*, which would carry 2,000 passengers, carried as many as 15,000 soldiers on any one voyage.

Donald Service was called up in September 1942 and became a driver with the RAF. He made many trips on board troop-carriers during the war, and describes the conditions that troops had to put up with:

> It was terrible on board. We were sleeping in canvas bunks six high. I got put into one three or four inches off the ground. I had my full pack, a rifle and a small kitbag, and the sergeant was packing us into the area. He said: 'Get in there and lie there until you get told to come out'. I looked at how I was gonna get down to that bed with all my kit. I packed my kitbag at the end, got my other kit on the other end and lay down on the floor and rolled into my bed. The next chap came in, got into the next bed and as he went in, his bed sagged into mine and I could hardly turn. I had to draw myself in to turn in the bed. We lay like that till we were called out. Once you were in, you couldn't move. You were allowed in turns to go up on deck to get some air.
>
> Once we were on board, we were watching them loading the other ships. You would have sworn they were going in one side and out the other. We were on it for five weeks. We washed in salt water. We got only one water-bottle a day filled with fresh water for cleaning our teeth and drinking.
>
> You could have cut it with a knife, the heat. I remember one night they put us on guard. I don't know what I was guarding! Sitting on a capstan, just hanging there, you just lost all your energy. You were given Vaseline to cover your bare parts for mosquitoes, and I put it on, but the cure was worse than the disease 'cos the sweat just ran off you down your arms and off your elbows. It was most uncomfortable. The best part was getting off it again.
>
> They talk about stress now, but you don't know what it is till you were treated like that. You were just packed in like cattle into those boats. It was a way of getting a big amount of men as far as possible as quick as they could.
>
> (BBC interview 2003)

Crossing the wide ocean – for love

While nineteenth-century economic emigrants constitute the single biggest group in Scotland's history, there were other groups of emigrants upon whom the spotlight has less often fallen.

Glasgow Museums: Museum of Transport.

During the Second World War, more than 100,000 British and European women are thought to have married Allied soldiers and sailors from Canada, the United States, Australia and New Zealand. They gained the nickname of 'War Brides', and thousands of them came from Scotland. The stories of them meeting their husbands and making the great sea journey to their new homes to raise families are a fascinating but generally untold chapter of twentieth-century Scottish history.

Johan DeWitt lived in Glasgow during the Battle of Britain, when German bombers made nightly sorties over the United Kingdom between August 1940 and September 1941. Her story has many of the characteristics of the stories of the War Brides [from Melynda Jarratt BA MA, Webmaster www.canadianbrides.com].

As one of the world's principal shipbuilding centres, Glasgow was an important target, and during the bombing there were many hundreds of fatalities and thousands of injuries. Few families escaped the disaster, and Johan knew many people who had been killed. The bombing campaign worked wonders, however, for government recruiters, with thousands anxious to join the war effort – and Johan joined the Women's Land Army, the government's solution to the shortage of agricultural workers with so many young men off fighting. It was while working on an isolated estate in Perthshire that Johan met her future husband, Luke DeWitt, a soldier with the Canadian Forestry Corps.

Cleaning a byre, up to her elbows in manure, Johan met Luke for the first time: 'I fell down and got in an awful mess, falling into the manure. I think to this day that Luke felt sorry for me! Maybe that's why he married me!' In

Canada's Immigration Museum – Pier 21 National Historic Site. Canada's 'front door' from 1928 to 1971 – point of arrival for war brides such as Johan DeWitt.

cing page: Glasgow Museums: useum of Transport.

February 1944, the young couple married, and their first child, Betty, was born in November. Eighteen months later, Johan started the long journey by train and 'war-bride' ship to Canada via London.

Johan's journey

'I was so thankful my daughter was toilet-trained. Washing the diapers in salt water, there were some sore wee bottoms.' One of Johan's abiding memories of the Atlantic crossing was the amount of zinc ointment that must have been used!

> After rations, the food was marvellous. We had roast beef and Yorkshire pudding, fish. You thought you'd died and gone to heaven. It was well into the voyage before I realised what I'd done, that there was a mighty big pond out there and I just couldn't swim back. But I had psyched myself up and I was ready for this, for better or worse. I hardly knew Luke. Last time I saw him he was in uniform, and here he was with a pin-striped suit and a blooming big fedora hat. I told him he looked like Al Capone.
>
> (BBC interview 2003)

Emigration remained at a high level until the end of the 1920s; but the Great Depression brought many back from America, where opportunities were scarce. By the second half of the twentieth century, the great era of emigration was effectively over. America and Canada had been pioneered and the cost of travel

Halifax, Nova Scotia.

Memorial of the Hector *landings, Pictou, Nova Scotia.*

had increased, largely due to the emergence of air traffic and the consequent reduction in the number of passenger ships. Says Marjory Harper:

> The legacy of Scottish emigration from a maritime perspective can be found in all the famous stories and in a global population of emigrant families. I think in the twenty-first century we have forgotten that Scotland was once a country that sent out large numbers of people on many, many emigrant ships. To our predecessors in the nineteenth century, and right up to the 1920s, the departure of emigrant vessels was big news and something that attracted the attention of newspapers and other commentators. Strangely, despite our huge maritime legacy, Scotland has not found a way to commemorate our emigrant past. In Ireland, Northern Ireland and Liverpool, and, of course, in Canada, Australia and the United States, they have. There was talk of a museum at the Tail of the Bank in the 1990s. This has never come to fruition.

Cameron

THIS STONE HAS BEEN ERECTED
TO THE GLORY OF GOD
AND
A MEMORIAL TO ALL NAMES LISTED
WHO IMMIGRATED FROM SCOTLAND
AND SETTLED IN NORTH AMERICA
CIRCA 18TH AND 19TH CENTURIES

CHAPTER 5

Men o' War and Safe Havens

How great was the *Michael*?

I n the sixteenth and seventeenth centuries, European monarchs had just begun to realise the significance of naval power – so they began to build powerful and prestigious flagships. One such king was James IV of Scotland. Unquestionably, in not only a Scottish but also a European context, the historic achievement of James IV was to take the two most impressive technologies that existed at the turn of the sixteenth century – big ships and big guns – and bring them together to create the *Michael*, a mould-breaking vessel designed around the principle of smashing other enemy vessels to splinters with shipboard cannon. The era of the ship as merely a high platform for bowmen was gone; and the *Michael*, launched in October 1511 in response to England's *Mary Rose*, could fairly be said to have been one of the first modern warships.

This impressive piece of naval engineering, with a superstructure as tall as a six-storey house, was a statement of Scottish nationhood and a warning against English aggression. She had been commissioned with the intention of leading a great crusade to the Holy Land, a crusade that James, a man not afraid to think big, intended should be led by the Auld Alliance – Scotland and France.

The neighbours were suitably impressed by James's new symbol of national and spiritual intent. The French ambassador who was entertained on board her in 1513 wrote that she was 'so powerful that another such would not be found in Christendom'. Henry VIII of England, never one to be outdone by his poor

The Michael *(model).*
© *The Trustees of the*
National Museums of
Scotland.

relations north of the Border, ordered the construction of the *Henri Grace à Dieu* – known as the *Great Harry* – in direct response.

The story of the *Michael* has a peculiarly Scottish outcome. James and his nobility perished on the field of Flodden in 1513 defending his French obligations. The *Michael* was then sold to Scotland's Gallic allies, for £18,000, principally because Scotland could not afford to operate such a prestigious vessel. Another reason for her sale was that the Regency which succeeded James did not share his enthusiasm for naval prowess. The *Michael* was a medieval white elephant. After thirty years of undistinguished service, she ended her days in France. Her biggest action had been a scarcely remembered skirmish at Carrickfergus in Ulster.

But could she really have been such a costly ship to build and run? Described as a 'veerie monstrous great ship', the *Michael* was, according to writer and lecturer Ian Morrison, at the upper end of the length practicable for wooden construction. Indeed, when the statistics relating to the *Michael* are laid out, the financial problems also become easier to understand.

Her construction at Newhaven, on the Forth, took five years, with the help of shipwrights from France. The final cost was put at £30,000, a fortune in the early sixteenth century and a significant proportion of the revenue of the Scottish crown. (At today's values, the *Michael* would have cost £14 million.) The chronicler Pitscottie also recorded that the project 'tuik so mekill timber that scho wastit all the wodis in Fyfe except Falkland Wood by [besides] all the tymmer that was gottin out of Norway'.

The four-masted vessel may have been up to 240 feet (75 metres) long, including bowsprit and additional rigging extensions. Her timber hull was probably at least five feet thick. Experts simply can't believe one report that the hull was ten feet thick. She carried twenty-seven large guns and hundreds of smaller artillery pieces. Apart from officers and master gunners, she had a crew of 300 men and 120 gunners and, in her fighting mode, was supplied with 3,000 gallons of ale, 240 salted beef carcasses, 5,300 salted fish, 13,000 loaves of bread and 200 stones of cheese, in addition to a wheen of fresh provisions.

Despite her inauspicious service record, the *Michael* was an impressive Scottish symbol. Three centuries were to pass before a ship of similar dimensions was constructed in Scotland. In those opening years of the sixteenth century, the project laid the foundations of Scotland's international reputation for brilliance in the art of shipbuilding.

The Royal Navy – a Scottish perspective from 1707

The idea of a naval base in Scotland was mooted as early as 1709, two years after the Act of Union, when the Firth of Forth was surveyed by Messrs Naish and Wood. Nothing was done, however; and no such facility would exist in Scotland until two centuries later, when the Rosyth naval base was constructed. For the naval strategist, Scotland is a gift. With its range of safe, secure deepwater anchorages, Scotland has been an excellent location for bases in both the ancient and modern contexts. The Scottish coastline commands the entrance into the North Sea and gives access to the North Atlantic and the Arctic Ocean as well as dominating key trade and fishing routes.

Since the Union, Scotland's role in British naval strategy has depended on the identity of the opposition. If the enemy were France, as it was for much of the

The Scottish coast is a gift for the naval strategist.

eighteenth and the early nineteenth century, then Scotland's naval function was generally peripheral. The wars against France were fought and co-ordinated from the south of England. However, in the twentieth century, when Germany and then the Soviet Union emerged as the opposition, Scotland's role was singularly important. Nowadays, the balance has, to a certain extent, shifted back south to Plymouth and Portsmouth, as naval targets now tend to be in far-flung places such as the Persian Gulf.

Throughout the eighteenth century, a naval career was a source of fame and fortune for a few admirals such Thomas Cochrane, 10th Earl of Dundonald, who served in locations as diverse as Chile and Greece. For many Scots, the British navy was quite simply the English navy, and for more than half a century the Jacobites regarded it as a means of their repression.

Professor Andrew Lambert, of the Department of War Studies, King's College, London, has no doubt that the political union of Scotland and England was the catalyst for a great change not only in the way in which naval power could be utilised but also in Scotland's prosperity. He says that, when the old frontiers disappeared, it allowed the energy of the state to be diverted outwards:

> It gave the British Empire the freedom from internal strife which is one of the key successes of the eighteenth and nineteenth centuries. It allowed Britain to focus those energies, those dynamic entrepreneurial energies outward, to conquer new worlds and to increase the trade coming in through all the great ports, not least Glasgow, in ships – many of them built on the Clyde, many of them crewed by Scots sailors, engineers, officers. So Scotland joins in the

great project of British Empire and from that extracts at least as much value as one might expect.

(BBC interview 2003)

During most of the nineteenth century, very few Scots joined the navy. One statistic puts the Scottish contingent in the Royal Navy during the nineteenth century at a very modest 4 per cent, although Scotland had 15 per cent of the United Kingdom's population. Naval officers were such an uncommon sight that it is said they were mistaken occasionally for Salvation Army officers or railway porters! A report from 1853 confirms this perception: 'little is comparatively known of the Royal Naval Service in Scotland, from whence we believe that a much larger number of excellent seamen might be obtained than at present'.

At the beginning of the nineteenth century, recruits from Scotland were said to have been 'deterred from joining by the great distance that separates their homes from existing naval bases'. But there were a few, as the possibly apocryphal story of the two Scottish sailors at Battle of Trafalgar in 1805 indicates. The men, from the same village, noticed Nelson's famous 'England expects ...' signal being run up. 'No mention there for auld Scotland', said one ruefully. 'Dinna worry, Alec,' says his pal, 'Scotland's sons know their duty. That's just a reminder to the Englishers to do theirs!'

Contact with the navy, as far as many parts of Scotland were concerned in the first half of the nineteenth century, was restricted to tours and exercises when the fleet called in at anchorages such as Brodick, Orkney and Invergordon. The arrival of the fleet was often celebrated, and its presence had a positive effect on the local economy for the duration of the stopover.

In 1859, the Royal Naval Volunteer Reserve was founded, and it proved considerably more successful in attracting Scots into service. They recruited professional seamen such as fishermen and ferrymen and trained them on older warships such as the *Unicorn* (the oldest British warship still afloat, now stationed at Dundee).

Although 'ironclads' were built on the Clyde in the 1860s, naval shipbuilding in Scotland did not take off in earnest until the Naval Defence Act of 1889, which laid out the government's declared aim of keeping Britain's navy at twice the size of its nearest competitors put together. The scale of the undertaking meant that contracts normally given exclusively to naval dockyards began to be awarded to private yards. In the years before the First World War, dreadnoughts, battleships and battle cruisers, with famous names such as *Colossus*, *Conqueror* and *Valiant*, rose on the stocks in Clyde yards such as Scott's, Beardmore's, John Brown's and Fairfield's.

THE NAVAL ESTIMATES: TYPES OF BATTLE-SHIPS, NEW AND OLD.

DRAWN BY F. T. JANE.

THE "GREAT MICHAEL."

A CONTRAST OF FOUR CENTURIES: TYPES OF THE PROJECTED GREAT SHIPS AND THE SCOTTISH WAR-SHIP "GREAT MICHAEL,"
ONE OF THE FIRST VESSELS BUILT AT ST. MARGARET'S HOPE, THE NEW NAVAL BASE

The battle-ships will be of no less than 18,000 tons, and will carry twelve big armour-piercing guns, besides many smaller. The cruisers will be of nearly 14,000 tons—which is heavier than most foreign battleships—and will carry among other ordnance six 9·2 in. armour-piercing guns. The new battle-ships, being without military tops and ventilator-cowls, will differ considerably in appearance from the general type of British battle-ship. Despite their immense size, they will be swifter and handier than any ships constructed before them. The "Great Michael," which was of some 1000 tons burden, was the monster ship of her day. She was built to compete with Henry the Seventh's "Great Harry," and was to a certain extent an armour-clad, for her sides on the water-line were 10 feet thick. Her career was short, as she foundered on her first sea-trip, and Scots' dreams of sea-power died with her.

With permission of the London Illustrated News Picture Library.

Faslane.

From 1914, production increased dramatically, and such yards were taken under the direct control of the Admiralty, almost ceasing merchant production. During the war years, a stunning 481 vessels were launched from the Clyde yards, including minesweepers and anti-submarine craft. The latter especially brought the smaller yards into the war effort.

The great sea fortress

Rosyth was the first new dockyard to be built in Britain since Portsmouth in 1690. The decision to go ahead came in response to the increasing likeliness of war with Germany in the opening years of the twentieth century. The First Sea Lord, Admiral Fisher, had reservations about the plan. He feared that the Forth was a potential trap should an enemy lay mines in the approaches or destroy the rail bridge and immobilise the entire fleet.

Nevertheless, work at Rosyth proceeded. The original plan was to build a base capable of holding a quarter of the fleet including a dockyard for ship repair, naval barracks and a victualling or supply base. However, extensive redevelopment of the bases on the south coast led to a modification of the plan, and expenditure was reduced. When completed, Rosyth was expected to house only one sixth of the fleet. The dockyard itself was heavily criticised, and, as a result of various delays, none of the facilities was in place when Britain entered the war in August 1914. Early in 1915, when it was realised that the war was likely to be a prolonged affair, efforts to complete the yard were accelerated.

The Battlecruiser Fleet, the most glamorous part of the navy, was situated there from early 1915; but, because the estuary gave the fleet no room for

127 THE SCOTS AT SEA

exercises that was safe from submarine attacks, they lacked gunnery practice. The dockyard was formally handed over to the navy in November 1917.

Scapa Flow, in Orkney, is perhaps one of the world's most famous naval anchorages. It had been recognised as a unique sanctuary as early as 1750 and was used during the Napoleonic Wars as an assembly point for ships sailing into the Baltic. Detailed soundings had been taken as early as 1812, during the war between Britain and America. Into the twentieth century, as allegiances changed, France and Britain drew together and Kaiser Wilhelm assembled his huge fleet. Scapa Flow then took on a crucial new importance. The Flow offered a unique set of opportunities; but, in particular, it could be utilised to control access to and from the North Sea. It was 'the stopper in the North Sea bottle'. Narrow entrances (none more than two miles wide) were seen as offering protection against submarine attack. To the south of the Flow, the racing tides of the Pentland Firth provided a natural defence at the gateway of the anchorage. The east-coast anchorages such as Harwich, the Humber and the Forth were not so suitable. The base was also close to the limit of the range of enemy submarines – but not beyond it as originally thought.

At the outbreak of the First World War, the Grand Fleet was sent north to Scapa, which was selected because it was so extensive. It offered sixty square miles of deep, sheltered anchorage capable of holding the entire fleet, surrounded by a ring of islands allowing the fleet to be protected from the worst of the weather and yet able to carry out exercises in complete security – to steam, to organise gunnery trials and to practise torpedo-running. Says Professor Andrew Lambert:

Scapa Flow, Orkney.

With a smaller fleet controlling the Straits of Dover, the Germans were now cut off from the rest of the world, and if they wanted to draw on its resources they would have to break the blockade; the Germans would have to fight a battle somewhere near Orkney, entirely to the advantage of the British and entirely to their own disadvantage. The use of Scapa Flow killed off any German attempt to have communication with the rest of the world.

The entire Grand Fleet, and 70,000 men, arrived on 29 July 1914, and Orkney was never to be the same again. At anchor, in Scapa Flow, it was a spectacular sight. At its peak of operation, the fleet was effectively a floating city consisting of 300 ships – battleships, cruisers, destroyers, support vessels, colliers, depot ships. It was the most powerful military force in the world with, according to Andrew Lambert, more guns than the Western Front and more firepower than all the armies fighting in the 'war to end all wars'. In an attempt to make the Flow even more secure, blockships were sunk in the narrow passages between the islands, and mines were laid. All the luxury fittings, including pianos and wardrobes, were landed to lighten the battleships in anticipation of a short and decisive victory – but the fleet was moored at Scapa for four years and fought only one major battle (see p. 132).

Orkney was not prepared for this 'invasion'. How could it be? Naval bases grow up around navies – not just the docks but also the pubs, the entertainment, all the things sailors look forward to when they come ashore. The green isles, a rural community with a very simple, hard but generally happy way of life, faced the daunting challenge of coping with the thousands of young men in their midst looking to fill their recreation time. The population of Orkney at the time was over 20,000, but it could increase by over 50,000 when the fleet was in. It is no surprise to learn that one mother is said to have kept her daughter locked in a back room for years, so worried was she about the hordes of young men wandering around Mainland, Orkney's principal island.

Lewis Munro, curator of the Scapa Museum at Lyness on the island of Hoy, on the western flank of the Flow, is the grandson of a sailor from HMS *Lion* who arrived with the Grand Fleet and made Orkney his permanent home. There were upwards of 20,000 sailors at Lyness alone during the First World War, and Lewis describes how a remarkable rapprochement was achieved, how Orkney welcomed the British navy and adjusted to the invasion which had landed in its midst:

Lots of men stationed here fell for local girls. There were ample opportunities to meet – dances put on by locals – in community halls and at the Cosmo ballroom. Also many families took in sailors – fed them and employed them. My grandfather, who had been a stonemason to trade, even did some work in that line while he was stationed here. My father came from Edinburgh and was a corporal in the Royal Marines. He was stationed at Scapa, got shore leave, met my mother and fell in love. It was the same story all over again.

(BBC interview 2003)

Lewis Munro.

Kirkwall, the islands' largest town, was transformed. During the First World War, sailors were based in camps away from the town. As a result of a strict rota of passes, chaos – and potential animosity – was avoided. Inevitably, incidents involving high-spirited or drunken sailors did happen, and a few of the more strait-laced folk of Orkney were offended. However, Orcadian farmers and retailers found themselves supplying a much-expanded local market and did well out of the friendly invasion. The Marquis of Zetland provided some land for football and golf, but there was often discontent among the soldiers and sailors. One young lieutenant wrote: 'for the first six months of the war we never saw a tree, a train or a woman'. Presumably there was no thought to order of preference in his remark!

Life on board ship in the Flow was a very austere business. The navy was obsessed with keeping its ships in good order: cleaning decks, painting and maintenance were part of the daily routine. Just like the men in the shore batteries, sailors would have to sit day after day in their gun emplacements – simply watching and waiting.

After the long hours of boredom, a report of the sighting of an enemy vessel was an event of major significance, as Orkney historian and folklorist Tom Muir relates:

> The story is told of someone spotting a German U-boat run aground
> on the Skerries just off the Flow. When the sighting was reported, the
> radio operator was asked: 'Are you sure it's not a whale?' His response:
> 'If it's a whale, it's got eighteen men sitting on its back waving!'
>
> (BBC interview 2003)

The Battle of Jutland

By 1916, the naval blockade of Germany from Scapa Flow was starting to have the desired effect, choking Germany's contact with possible allies in the outside world. The Germans were being starved towards submission, their crisis compounded by the fact that so many of their men had left the agricultural industry to fight on the Western Front.

With their High Seas Fleet penned into the Baltic and the southern reaches of the North Sea, the German High Command devised a plan to lure the British fleet into battle to break the stranglehold. They were pragmatic enough to know that they would not defeat the entire British navy; but their goal was to limit the effectiveness of the British Grand Fleet and to punch a hole in the blockade to give Germany access to the outside world.

Admiral Scheer was Commander-in-Chief of the German High Seas Fleet, comprising almost 100 warships. He began sorties against cities along England's eastern coast in an attempt to lure the British Fleet out towards his waiting U-boats. By 30 May 1916, the British Admiralty had wind of the plan and put the Grand Fleet to sea under Lord Jellicoe in an effort to gain the initiative.

Sailing from Scapa Flow and Cromarty, the main fleet was to rendezvous with the battlecruisers under Admiral Beatty from their base at Rosyth on the Forth. The British fleet, with superiority in numbers, successfully evaded the U-boats. The Germans sighted only a handful of ships, leading them to think that the Grand Fleet had not been put to sea. On the afternoon of 31 May, about 100 miles west of Jutland, a Danish merchant ship sailed unwittingly between the opposing fleets, prompting both sides to investigate and thereby bringing the two navies within sight of each other for the first time. The Battle of Jutland, the only Great Fleet battle of the First World War, began accidentally.

The fighting started with small cruisers and then extended to the battle-cruiser fleet, and then all the battle fleets became engaged. As the writer and former naval attaché James Davidson wrote, the visibility was poor, signalling was difficult and orders were confused. There were genuine problems in trying to establish whether the grey shapes looming out of the murk were British or German. The conflict unfolded in four or five phases. Admiral Beatty's battle-cruiser force sighted their opposite numbers and turned quickly to pursue the Germans, who in turn fled south towards their High Seas fleet. This led Beatty towards the destruction that the Germans had planned for him. Two of his ships were hit; they blew up and sank with enormous loss of life.

Then Beatty turned and led the Germans north towards Jellicoe's forces, where the Kaiser's fleet was heavily bombarded and fled into the North Sea. Jellicoe's vessels now stood between the German fleet and Germany and were ready for what might have proved to be one of the most decisive battles in British naval history. However, there was a breakdown in communications between the Admiralty and the British fleet during the night, and the German fleet was able to squeeze through the back door and find its way home to its North Sea bases. Says Professor Andrew Lambert:

> It was inconclusive tactically, but the strategic results of Jutland were enormous. The Germans never again thought about challenging for command of the sea; they gave up any idea that they could beat the Royal Navy and they turned their efforts to restricted submarine warfare, which brought the Americans into the war and very quickly led to Germany's defeat.

Professor Lambert believes that the British Navy won the Battle of Jutland. The Germans claimed victory, as they sank more ships; but Lambert believes that that is an irrelevant measure and insists that in battle the winner is the team that stays on the field and waits for the next round. Unequivocally, he states:

> The Germans ran away. The British stayed and were ready to fight the next day. The defeat of the German High Seas Fleet at Jutland is apparent from the fact that they opted for submarine warfare. That was the most clear, unequivocal demonstration of their defeat.

Winston Churchill, who was the First Sea Lord in 1915, described the battle as 'the culminating manifestation of naval force in the history of the world' at a time when many people thought Jutland was a defeat for the Royal Navy. The historian and military strategist, Basil Liddell Hart, however, writing after the war, claimed that the impact of Jutland on the course of the war was 'negligible'. Liddell Hart served in the trenches, and his experience of the slaughter led him to criticise the conduct of that war and to develop a strategy which brought together armoured units, artillery, infantry and aircraft in decisive attacks of overwhelming strength.

After the battle, Lord Jellicoe was criticised for not pursuing the Germans more vigorously; but the actions of the fleet were in accordance with the tactical doctrine that Jellicoe had agreed with the Admiralty. Jellicoe's battle orders ensured centralised control of the fleet, and, once in place, it was difficult to see Jutland coming to a different conclusion. Where Britain probably blundered was in allowing the public-relations initiative to slip away immediately after Jutland. Germany quickly issued press statements claiming a major victory; and the Admiralty, with a very aloof and supercilious attitude, was slow to respond, causing many people in the United Kingdom in the aftermath of the battle to believe that the war was all but lost.

While the arguments of the naval tacticians still resound, it is important to consider what sort of hell the ordinary seamen experienced in the course of this battle. Naval conflict in the first years of the twentieth century had changed markedly from Nelson's day, a century before, when the action was generally at close quarters. The enemy in those days was visible for the sailors, who were operating in a fairly open space; they could see much of what was going on along the decks and would have had a sense of the manoeuvring of the enemy.

In the twentieth century, men worked in the depths of the ships, in engine rooms, in the magazines and in the support systems within the vessel. They knew that the guns were firing, and they knew that the ship had been hit. But it was very difficult for the ordinary seamen to have a clear vision of what was happening; even the admirals were struggling to see exactly what was taking place.

At Jutland, this problem was exacerbated by fog, by the very thick smoke from burning coal and from the vast amount of cordite that was used in the guns as propellant for the shells. Everybody was operating in a zone of restricted visibility. And the action happened very rapidly. Three of the big British ships blew up and all but a handful of their crew were killed before they sank. Most men would have died very quickly, but others would have had terrible flash burns or shrapnel injuries.

the war have again and again proved the excellence of
our command, and all ranks of our crews and the
material of the ships, the great sea battle gave them
the opportunity to display fully all their excellent
qualities, which the German nation already in peace
time considered as a definite national asset of the
highest value in the case of war.

BRITANNIA NO LONGER RULES THE WAVES.

In the Berlin *Lokalanzeiger* Captain von
Kuehlwetter, comparing the qualities of the
vessels engaged in the battle, says :—

Great Britain has used her older vessels in the
distant theatres of war, and has lost many of them.
This permits the conclusion that the Home Fleet is
composed only of the latest and best vessels. The
superior number of the British ships must not be forgotten, even if the whole of the German High Sea
Fleet had participated in the fight. German sailors
have never underestimated the British Fleet, but
have considered it the best of all the foreign fleets.
To-day we know that we can accomplish more than
the British. Great Britain is not what she believed
herself to be nor what she endeavoured to appear.
The German success gives the death blow to the
Anglo-Saxon idea that Great Britain is the ruler of
the seas.

The *Lokalanzeiger* estimates the total German
loss in ships at 23,056 tons, as compared with a
British loss of 133,210 tons. The *Tageblatt*
estimates that the German loss of great battle-
ships amounts to 13,200 tons, as against 102,980
tons lost by the British. The newspaper continues :—"The British losses represent no
decisive factor, but a severe blow." Other
papers point out that both fleets were beyond
reach of their bases, and so had to rely on their
own strength.—*Reuter.*

"WHERE WERE THE BRITISH?"

The *Kölnische Volkszeitung*, commenting on
the British Admiralty *communiqué* concerning
the naval battle, writes :—

We see with surprise that the German sea forces
avoided prolonged fighting and yet the battle lasted
some 20 hours. Where, then, were the British main

Before 1914, fully equipped hospital ships normally stayed with the fleet and kept the wounded on board as long as necessary. However, during the First World War, the number of injured increased, dramatically altering the role of hospital ships to that of casualty clearing stations transferring the wounded back to the shore bases. At the time of the Battle of Jutland, casualties were transferred to naval hospital ships anchored in the Firth of Forth. Professor Lambert summarises the conditions faced by the sailors during the Battle of Jutland:

> It would have been a grim, alien experience. The men are shut away in a box with lots of activity all around them. The only thing they've got to keep them going is their job. And the more professional and committed they are, the less their mind might wander and ponder the very real danger with which they were faced. That professional, organised, disciplined response was the key to the successful battle performance. At Jutland, both sides demonstrated these qualities. They were both well-trained, professional fighting forces. So we don't get mass panic, we don't get men refusing to do their duty. On both sides, the men did what was expected of them.

Scuttling the High Seas Fleet

When the Armistice was signed on 11 November 1918, one of the conditions was that the German fleet would be interned. Scapa Flow was the obvious place

The German fleet at Scapa. Reproduced with kind permission of the Orkney Library and Archive.

Facing page: The Times, *3 June 1916. Reproduced with permission.*

Germans after defeat.
The Imperial War Museum.

for such a vast undertaking, as it was a large anchorage where, under the guns of the British, a watchful eye could be kept on the subdued Imperial fleet.

The actual surrender of the German fleet became a triumphant passage of conquest, with the Germans being asked to steam between two lines of British warships at a rendezvous point off the Firth of Forth. This was the biggest concentration of large ships the world had seen, some 250 ships in all. It was a time of humiliation for the Germans, as the Royal Navy celebrated what many experts consider to have been Britain's greatest naval triumph. As they arrived in Scapa Flow, the names of some of the great German warships would have been familiar to the people of Orkney from the tales of the action at Jutland. Before long, names such as the *Kronprinz Wilhelm* entered Orkney folklore.

The fleet was effectively being held hostage for the good behaviour of Germany and for a final settlement in the Versailles peace process. The men on the ships were, quite naturally, desperate to get home. Germany was in turmoil, the Imperial government had fallen, there were revolutionary outbreaks and, for the Germans in particular, the future was filled with uncertainty. To add to the tension, the men were locked away, refused shore leave for months on end, could not swap ships and were refused supplies. It must have seemed a bleak and wild environment, which at the best of times even the British soldiers found difficulty in enthusing over. There had been mutinies on board most of the larger German ships by a movement like a 'people's soviet' of soldiers and sailors.

The German High Seas Fleet.
With permission of ITN.

Some commanders had to be moved to smaller vessels for their own safety, including the admiral in charge, von Reuter. He worked hard to keep the lid on what was a powder-keg situation, when his men refused to clean the ships or recognise the authority of officers. In this atmosphere, it is hardly surprising that a last-ditch plan for a 'death or glory' attack on the British Fleet was abandoned.

The scuttling of the German High Seas Fleet. Reproduced with kind permission of the Orkney Library and Archive.

The senior officers were anxious to salvage German pride, and the ordinary sailors simply wanted to get back to their families. When the order finally came to scuttle the fleet, to steal Britain's moment of glory, there must have been almost unanimous agreement to do the deed. With chaos surrounding the peace talks, von Reuter waited until the British fleet left Scapa on their regular manoeuvres on 21 June 1919. Convinced that they would return to seize the fleet finally, he raised the flag at 10 a.m. to signal the start of the scuttling – and, all across the Flow, the bells rang out signalling 'abandon ship'. At noon, the *Friedrich der Grosse* became the first ship to roll over. The last ship to go down was the *Hindenburg* around 5 p.m. It was a final, almost Wagnerian act of defiance.

A group of Stromness schoolchildren, on a boat trip around the Fleet that morning, found themselves close-quarter witnesses to this dramatic episode in maritime history. On board the *Kestrel*, they saw ships turning over all around them – a dangerous and unforgettable experience.

The last direct casualties of the First World War are said to have been nine German sailors fleeing their ships, shot by British marines who watched incredulously as the fleet sank before their eyes. An unknown number of Germans drowned. Most of the sunken fleet was salvaged between the wars, and only four light cruisers and three battleships remain on the bed of the Flow, targets today for sport divers.

Training for the Battle of the Atlantic

The sea war in 1939–45 was, for the most part, fought in convoys and through amphibious landings. It was in this battle arena that the Firth of Clyde, and

Scapa: Bayern 1. *Reproduced with kind permission of the Orkney Library and Archive.*

the west of Scotland generally, came to play a leading role. Not until 1940, when the great German war machine swept across Belgium and France, did it become apparent that highly specialised naval training, which previously had been undertaken in the south of England, would have to find a new home at a distance from the main theatre of war. In addition, the west-coast waterways were overcrowded – so two completely new military ports were built in the west of Scotland, at Faslane and at Loch Ryan near Stranraer. When France fell to the Germans, it was decided that these two ports should operate exclusively for troops and supplies.

While basic training continued at bases in the south, the west coast of Scotland was quickly identified as the most suitable location for training in the skills of naval aviation, submarine and amphibious warfare. The advantages here were many. It was remote from air raids and from the sorties of German submarines. The coast was well endowed with remote and empty beaches and harbours where seamen could act out landing and invasion techniques well away from prying eyes. The Clyde estuary is also close to transport systems and industrial resources with a wealth of remote harbours and anchorages.

The Admiralty was aware that a 'working-up' base would be required to prepare the men for the rigours of the war at sea. A plan to locate this base on the Lorient coast of France was abandoned after France fell. With the Germans now using the French ports, all the possible south-of-England sites – Bristol, Portsmouth, Southampton and Plymouth – were within easy reach of enemy firepower. The west of Scotland provided the answer. The waters of the Western Isles are deep, ideal for exercises and for challenging the navigational skills of the mariners. Not the least important consideration was that it kept the sailors away from the many distractions of city life.

- Scapa had its moments of tragedy as well as high drama during the First World War. A few days after the Battle of Jutland, the cruiser **Hampshire** left Scapa carrying Field Marshall Lord Kitchener on a special mission to Russia. Just off Marwick Head, on Orkney's rugged west coast, the ship struck a mine and was lost with all hands.

- In July 1917, the 22,900-ton **Vanguard** was at anchor in the Flow when her magazine exploded. Only three men survived.

- In August of that year, Commander Edwin Dunning achieved naval aviation history when he landed his Sopwith Pup aeroplane on the foredeck of the **Furious**. Men on board grabbed the wings to stop the plane from going overboard. The next day, Dunning attempted the feat again and was killed.

- During the Second World War, when Scapa was used once again to blockade the North Sea and allow quick and easy access to the North Atlantic, there was another major disaster when a German submarine, U-47, slipped between the blockships and sank the Jutland veteran **Royal Oak** with the loss of 833 men. This resulted in the construction of the Churchill Barriers linking the string of islands on the eastern flank of the Flow.

During the course of the war, there are thought to have been as many as forty bases operating up and down the west coast of Scotland, effectively turning the area into one vast naval training camp. In towns along the west coast, hotels were taken over as messes, offices and training bases. Largs, for example, was the main training centre for amphibious warfare; Campbeltown housed the main anti-submarine training base.

HMS *Western Isles*, a converted ferry moored at Tobermory on Mull with its charismatic commanding officer, Admiral Sir Gilbert Stephenson – 'Puggy' to his peers – was perhaps the most colourful and famous of these bases. From 1940, the crews of 1,132 ships destined for combat in the Battle of the Atlantic were trained here.

Admiral Stephenson was born in 1878, and his naval career spanned an era of great change. He saw action in the Dardanelles during the First World War,

THE SCOTS AT SEA

and after the war he advocated the use of new techniques to tackle the growing menace of submarines. He was soon widely recognised as the navy's leading expert on anti-submarine warfare. With the outbreak of the Second World War, he was in charge of convoys; then, drawing on his experience fighting submarines, he was given the task of leading anti-submarine patrols between Scotland and Norway.

The job facing Admiral Stephenson at Tobermory was a daunting one. Hundreds of vessels, many built on the Clyde, were commissioned to fight the U-boats. They often reached Tobermory with only a few key servicemen who had any combat experience. Such was the pressure to get the ships out and operating that Admiral Stephenson had only fourteen days to prepare the trainees for action. The training was as unconventional as it was intensive, and Stephenson is remembered for using all his energy, determination and imagination in preparing them for what they would face in the Atlantic.

Most of the officers and crews arriving in Tobermory had never been to sea before; but Stephenson had a code of practice that enabled him to perform miracles. His bywords were *spirit* – a determination to win; *discipline* – it was no good being the finest men in the world if you were not going to obey orders; *administration* – making sure the work of the ship was evenly divided, that meals were in the right place at the right time, that the whole organisation of the ship was both stable and elastic; and *technique* – how to use the equipment. Most of all, the Admiral taught the seamen what they might expect in battle – the heat, the noise, the smoke – and the absolute necessity in a situation which might change every five seconds for quick reactions, to give and obey orders. Stephenson was constantly aware that he was trying to

Tobermory, Mull.

THE SCOTS AT SEA   **140**

give to men with no knowledge of the sea the expertise which had taken him decades to acquire.

One important consideration that he stressed again and again was to expect the unexpected, which he saw as the essence of battle. During scheduled classes on aircraft recognition, depth-charge drills or communications training, the Commodore would stage one of his 'emergencies' ranging from a man overboard to a fire below decks. Occasionally, a captain would be informed his ship was sinking! When the seamen began to struggle in the face of constructed catastrophe, Stephenson would advise: 'Improvise, my boy, improvise!' A favourite trick of his was to sneak up on a boat in the dead of night – and, if he were not hailed, he would board and remove a vital piece of equipment, displaying it to the entire base in the morning. Many a shame-faced captain would be called to account for his carelessness in this manner.

Author and former BBC newsreader Richard Baker, who has written a book about Admiral Stephenson, went to Tobermory for training in 1944. The Battle of the Atlantic was supposed to be past its zenith, but there was still considerable U-boat activity. He recalls seeing the *Queen Elizabeth* and *Queen Mary* in their 'war paint' in the Firth of Clyde, and his first encounter with the 'old boy' was equally memorable:

> There was a rather wild party for my nineteenth birthday at Tobermory during which I got gentian violet ointment all over my face; I was completely mauve. For a joke, my captain sent me with a message to Admiral Stephenson on his headquarters ship. I had to face this fierce old gentleman who wanted to know my job on

Richard Baker.

board. I told him I was assistant gunnery officer and sports and entertainments officer. 'Oh, I see you take the second part of your job very seriously!' declared the admiral.

(BBC interview 2003)

Richard Baker believes that the 'Terror of Tobermory' image that Stephenson adopted was very much for the benefit of the seamen:

> It was his business to instil a bit of fear of damnation into people – and, as a matter of fact, all of us were rather more scared of him than we were of the prospect of the U-boats and the Battle of the Atlantic. Quite glad to get away, really.

Stephenson realised that he was training civilians to become sailors, but stood by his motto which was impressed on all recruits no matter how inexperienced: 'ship first, shipmates second, yourself last'.

Relationships with the folk of Mull were good. The Commodore ensured that fetes, parties and church sermons were all well attended, and he worked hard to make certain that the people of Tobermory were not put out by the presence of HM Navy. There was little time off for the men, such was the intensity of the work schedule during their short stay. It was freely admitted after the war that the 'working-up' methods developed at Tobermory provided the foundation for such training throughout the navy. Admiral Sir John Casper, First Sea Lord, commented: 'To train raw recruits to an adequate standard to face the U-boat was really impossible, and yet after they'd left Tobermory no one ever found fault with them'.

Boarding the Shetland Bus

Scotland was riddled with secret bases like Tobermory; many of them offered a haven to European resistance fighters. With Shetland's proximity to occupied Norway, the North Sea became a lifeline for resistance fighters and refugees in an operation called 'The Shetland Bus'.

For weeks following the German invasion of Norway, in April 1940, a fleet of up to thirty fishing vessels crossed the North Sea to Shetland bringing British military personnel and some 200 Norwegian refugees. Many of these vessels, in the guise of ordinary fishing boats, returned in a secret undercover operation to embark more refugees and to bring out Norwegian volunteers for the Allied forces.

An underground network of some complexity was soon operating in Norway, with thousands of servicemen hiding out in the mountains in immediate and desperate need of arms and communication systems. Because of Shetland's close geographical proximity, it became the natural base for underground agents heading for Norway. In November 1940, a British major, L.H. Mitchell, was ordered to Shetland to organise a regular undercover link between Norway and Shetland, setting up a line of communication for couriers, saboteurs, radio operators and weapons instructors in support of the Norwegian resistance.

The first operation took place just before Christmas 1940 with the landing of an agent near Bergen, and twelve more trips followed until suspended for the summer months of 1941, when the long hours of daylight meant that the network was dangerously exposed. By this time, the little secret navy had expanded to twelve fishing vessels.

Lunna Voe, in the north of the islands, was established as base of operations in 1941, and, from here, many small-scale missions were successfully carried out. Using the small fishing cutters, Norwegians landed agents, radio sets and ammunition. They returned to the Voe with refugees.

Because of its exposed position and the difficulty in carrying out repairs to the boats, the base moved to Scalloway, on Shetland's west coast, in 1942. The local firm of William Moore & Sons, with forty years' engineering experience, took on the repairs, and a new slipway was built.

From Kergord House, called Flemington until 1945, Major Mitchell ran the show. One floor of the building was a dormitory for Norwegian agents waiting to sail or to be debriefed. Close liaison was kept with local navy commanders to ensure that the operations of the 'Bus' did not clash with destroyer sweeps, motor torpedo-boat raids or RAF depth-charging. The work, which included maintenance of wireless equipment and production of sabotage gear, took place by the light of erratic wind-powered electricity and paraffin lamps.

As well as suffering the severe winter weather, the crews and their passengers were always at risk from German planes and ships. The single biggest loss was in November 1941, when the *Blia* went down with the loss of all forty-three on board. During the winter of 1942–3, the unit suffered serious losses – ten vessels, forty-four crew members and more than sixty refugees were killed either by storms or by German attacks. From 1943, the 'Bus' operation became part of the Royal Norwegian Navy as a special unit, popularly known as 'The Shetland Gang'.

Scalloway Harbour.

Andreas Færøy was an engineer with the Shetland Bus who saw the aim of the operations quite clearly – keeping up the spirit of the Norwegian people until liberation. The Bus, he believes, did exactly that. However, danger was ever-present. Andreas describes how, on one occasion, his boat was attacked by two German fighter planes. In the exchange of fire with the aircraft, Andreas was convinced that one plane was so badly damaged that it would never have made it back to base. Before their return to Shetland, a dramatic adventure awaited.

> We took to the lifeboat off the Norwegian coast, but the boat had to be repaired because it had been peppered by all kinds of projectiles. We rowed south down the coast – some of us were badly hurt – and

Andreas Færøy.

we had to hide for a few days, moving from place to place. We later learned that there was a reward out for us, although it was a pretty small one; anyone who turned us in would have got less for us than they would for selling one decent pig on the black market!

(BBC interview 2003)

Following the 1943 setbacks, the closure of the base was mooted but, instead, fresh backing came in the shape of three well-armed US navy motor torpedo boats with a top speed of twenty-two knots – the *Hitra*, *Hessa* and *Vigra*. During the last season, 1944–5, eighty trips were made by the 'Bus', seventy-six of them successfully. The *Hitra* has since been completely restored by the Norwegian navy.

Barbara Melkevic's husband, Orne, was also an engineer with the Bus and made fifteen secret missions on fishing boats, spiriting agents and supplies into Norway and bringing out refugees. Wives and girlfriends of the Bus crewmen were told that their partners' work was not to be spoken about. Women had no idea how long the trips would last, and Barbara recalls going down to the harbour to count the boats, wondering when her man would return. The anxiety was fully justified because, apart from the dangers at sea, if they were caught they faced instant execution. Barbara explains:

> During that last winter, when fishing boats were used, seven boats didn't come back. We couldn't ask questions, of course, but we noticed that men were missing, not coming to the dances. We were a group of girls, and being able to speak to each other was a help. It

Barbara Melkevic.

was a very, very difficult time, but it was something you simply had
to cope with. There was nothing else to do. I stayed in my father's
house when Orne was away, and we had a garden – potato, crops,
vegetables which we grew. I did a lot of knitting and that sort of
thing. Time just slipped away.

(BBC interview 2003)

Barbara says her husband was simply happy to be helping with the war effort.
Orne was from the village of Telebok, which was later burned by the Germans
as a centre of resistance activity; the women and children were interned and
the men were sent to German concentration camps. Before that event, Orne
visited his home village twice on Bus operations, calling in briefly to see his
sister and her children.

One of the most famous operations undertaken by the Norwegian Naval
Independent Unit under British command was an attempt to sink the German
battleship *Tirpitz*. On 26 October 1942, a fishing boat called the *Arthur* left
Shetland under the command of Norwegian Leif 'Shetlands' Larsen, a man whose
name is synonymous with the Shetland Bus, and sailed towards Trondheimfjord
where the *Tirpitz* was anchored. At 42,000 tons, *Tirpitz* was the pride of the
German Fleet, the largest warship ever built in Germany and a constant threat
to supply lines between the Western Allies and the Soviets.

The nineteen-metre *Arthur* made the hazardous voyage to Norway carrying
a decoy cargo of peat to disguise the remarkable weapons it had on board
– two 'human torpedoes' known as chariots. The chariot was designed for the
crew to sit astride wearing diving suits; and on its nose was a large detachable
warhead. The plan was for the two-man crew to steer below the *Tirpitz*, attach
the warhead to the underside of the ship and make their escape on the body of
the chariot. With only a few miles to go to the target, a violent storm caused
the chariots to break loose from the *Arthur* and the mission had to be aborted.
The *Arthur* was scuttled and the crew was forced to flee.

Peterhead, in Aberdeenshire, played a separate role as a base to transport
agents for the Secret Intelligence Service. Again, Norwegian fishing vessels were
used; and Peterhead, at the peak of operations, ran eight fishing cutters.

A very different kind of war

In 1939, the main submarine base for Scotland was located at Dundee, where
ten boats were stationed. However, it was the waters of the Clyde which were
seen as ideal for submarine manoeuvres, although it was not until the Second
World War had passed into history, and the Cold War began, that Faslane and

Scalloway Pier.

the Holy Loch, both used previously for warships, would be considered as submarine bases.

The introduction, by the mid-1950s, of first the atomic bomb and then the hydrogen bomb completely changed the defence priorities for Britain and brought Scotland spectacularly into the international spotlight. Another Battle of the Atlantic was unlikely, and strategic interest shifted to monitoring the Atlantic for Soviet submarines and warships.

It was thought from a very early stage that the only way in which the United Kingdom could defend herself from nuclear attack was to have the capability to hit back hard enough to persuade any enemy to think twice about launching a missile assault. In effect, it was a policy designed to create a nuclear stand-off. The Cold War was born. Old bases like Scapa Flow and Invergordon closed, and the navy concentrated on the west coast.

The Polaris missile programme gave Britain the facility to threaten a range of cities in the vast Soviet Union. It was not overwhelming force, and wasn't even enough to menace the Soviet Union's integrity, but it proved to be a sufficient deterrent. According to Professor Andrew Lambert, the Polaris system was very cheap, very effective and a very successful deterrent.

The original Polaris missile had a range of 1,500 miles, which was an enormous technological advance. For a British submarine to hit a Russian city, however, it needed to get into the North Atlantic and into an area from which it could make that range. They also needed to get to that station as quickly as possible. Establishing a base in Scotland allowed the submarines to reach the stations swiftly compared with existing naval facilities in England. Faslane on the Gare Loch quickly came into the equation.

The waters of the Gare Loch are deep, and the passages to the north and west through the Minches and the Kyle of Lochalsh provide excellent training waters and relative discretion. Unlike the warships of old, such as the *Michael*, which were designed to strike awe into the hearts of the enemy by their visible presence, submarines have to operate by stealth.

The Faslane area, beautifully situated on the sea loch, had been a pleasant residential area for successful Glasgow businessmen; but, during the Second World War, the need for secure bases away from the ever-present threat of bombing in the south saw the district transformed. After the Second World War, there had been much debate about its future. The north end of the base became a breaker's yard while, in the south end, little of note happened until 1954 when a fuelling base for hydrogen-peroxide-powered submarines was constructed. The base grew from nothing in the early 1960s to the enormous industrial site of today: jam-packed with engineering facilities, training simulators, offices and workshops.

Because of the limited range of the missiles, the Americans also needed a base on the west coast of Scotland. They arrived at the Holy Loch in 1961 and stayed until 1992. Their presence made them an obvious target for anti-war protesters throughout that period, and this action has continued into the twenty-first century at Faslane. However, the economic impact on the area of the Holy Loch base was huge, and Dunoon was said to have had the highest proportion of taxi-drivers in Europe.

Once the British Polaris programme began, in 1963, the Faslane base expanded dramatically. Other sites were considered, such as Falmouth and Milford Haven, but the Ministry of Defence wanted a deep anchorage and easy

Faslane.

access to open seas, and they already owned the land at Faslane. With industrial decline beginning to be felt on Clydeside, there were also political considerations. From a few jetties that had been left by the army, the entire Faslane base was constructed in five years.

When Britain's first nuclear-armed Polaris submarine, HMS *Resolution*, entered service in 1967, it was seen by the establishment as a powerful demonstration of Britain's capability to play a role in international affairs, even in the much-changed world of the Cold War. But the anti-Polaris protests continued.

Mike Henry, one of the captains of the Resolution *in 1967.*

The role of these 'deterrent' submarines was completely new, totally the reverse of the aggressive hunter-killer role played previously by submarines. The Polaris/Trident subs spend their patrol at sea effectively hiding, disappearing for weeks and months. In this period, the only people who know their location are the commanding officer and the navigation officer. Naval sources have described these submarines as the ultimate stealth weapon.

Captain Mike Henry, one of the two captains of the *Resolution*, recalls testing the Polaris system and the sensation as the very first missile left the submarine:

> You got a sort of thump as the missile went, and that was a great relief. In fact, I think my most nervous moment was after I had said 'You have the captain's permission to fire', and turned my little key. I knew my missile officer had his trigger to pull – and when he pulled it, if nothing happened, then it really would have been extremely embarrassing. I mean, it would have been a disaster! But it went perfectly and landed within the prescribed area down range.
>
> (BBC interview 2003)

The Polaris system set the United Kingdom apart. Britain was regarded as more powerful than other states in Europe. It was also seen by some as justification for Britain's seat on the Security Council at the United Nations and gave her international clout. Britain, with her deterrent force operating out of the Clyde, was for a time one of the Big Three – along with the United States and the Soviet Union – one of the key international players. In the second half of the twentieth century, possession of Polaris became a key part of Britain's identity. Since 1967, there has not been a day when a nuclear submarine has not been at sea in the defence of the United Kingdom.

After more than thirty years of service, the Polaris missile system and the submarines that carried it were superseded by new technology, and replacements were considered. Britain was also able to acquire the Trident system from the United States, the same source as Polaris. The construction of the submarine *Vanguard* to carry the new missiles restated British determination to look after herself.

Professor Andrew Lambert sees the selection of the name *Vanguard* for the first new V-class vessel as having been enormously important. He explains:

> This is a ship name with a history going back to the Armada campaign. There have been *Vanguards* at all the great battles. It was Nelson's flagship at the Battle of the Nile, there was one at Jutland, and the last battleship built on the Clyde was HMS *Vanguard*. It is a name with a huge history, so the navy is tying itself into the preservation of that deterrence. It is investing its own credibility in that system. These aren't numbered units. These are ships with names, with histories, with identities. So you're linking the navy to the mission, to the national identity and to the longer-term preservation of Britain's international standing.

The Trident system gave Britain a nuclear deterrent based under the sea with a longer range and far more warheads. Ironically, before the missile came into service, the Soviet Union disappeared and some of the rationale for the system went with it. But who knows what the world political map will look like in twenty years?

Commodore John Borley ADC, director of HM Naval Base Clyde, believes that because the present Trident system has the capacity to inflict vastly greater devastation than was caused at Hiroshima, it is inconceivable that we would ever actually use it. Like most of us, Commodore Borley wonders just how easy or difficult it would be to press the button should a catastrophic scenario develop:

> I'm sure it's very difficult. I actually don't know the command and control processes that lie behind the button because I don't need to know ... that decision could only come from the very, very highest authority in the land.

(BBC interview 2003)

According to Professor Lambert, it makes sense for the United Kingdom to keep and use this system as the basis of her national security policy. The bottom line seems to be that the Royal Navy's Faslane base on the Clyde, with the entire complex infrastructure to service the submarines well established, is likely to be home to the British nuclear deterrent for a very long time to come.

CHAPTER 6

Steamboats, Puffers and Blockade-busters

Keeping the paddles turning

On the opening page of Book Four of *Lanark*, Alasdair Gray's epic Scottish novel of the 1980s, there is a fantastic panorama of Scotland which captures everything from North Sea oil rigs to the tower of the University of Glasgow. Look carefully: in the busy Clyde estuary you will spot a paddle steamer cracking on towards Dunoon. That paddle steamer can only be the *Waverley*, known to her legions of fans as the last sea-going paddle steamer in the world.

The Waverley. *Reproduced with kind permission of Waverley Excursions Ltd.*

Almost as many Scots now go to Dallas as go to Dunoon, or to Rome as to Rothesay; yet this ship, with her red, white and black twin funnels leaning back at a rakish angle, her paddles churning up the foam, flags snapping in the breeze and decks crowded with excited sightseers, is an important summer tourist attraction for the west of Scotland. The ship also seems to hold a special fascination for Clydesiders: she is a link with an almost-vanished maritime past.

The name is taken from the series of novels by Sir Walter Scott, a rich source of names for generations of Clyde steamers. Other steamships named from this source included the *Jeanie Deans, Marmion, Lucy Ashton, Lorna Doone* and *Talisman*. It is important to remember that these were hard-working commercial ships and not tourist attractions. It was only in later years that they began to acquire celebrity status.

At Dunkirk, in 1940, another paddle steamer named *Waverley* was sunk while taking part in the evacuation. She was replaced by a new *Waverley* in 1947. The post-war *Waverley* began service on the route from Craigendoran near Helensburgh, effectively the London and Northern Eastern Railway's headquarters on the River Clyde, to Arrochar, at the head of Loch Long. The lochside villages had not seen a steamer service since the war began in 1939, so the *Waverley*'s arrival was a big day for the estuary, a day when communities began to look to a brighter future.

All eyes were on the vessel, and for weeks the press was filled with comment, both negative and positive, debating the lines, performance and significance of the newcomer. However, the consensus of opinion was that the *Waverley*,

---

At the races

Paddle-steamer racing on the Clyde was at its keenest in the Victorian era and had its roots purely in commercial competition. The faster the vessel, the quicker you got to your holiday destination – so companies vied to outdo each other. Success often depended simply on how quickly the stokers could get coal into the furnaces. Rivalry between skippers was also intense, and cutting each other up in the approaches to piers was dangerously commonplace. Alan Jamieson, current skipper of the **Waverley**, is glad those days are gone: 'You might keep the speed on to the very last minute when approaching the berth, hoping your helmsman and engineer were in good form, because when you ring astern you're going to need to stop!' The evidence is that this did not always happen!

The Waverley. *Reproduced with kind permission of Waverley Excursions Ltd.*

although an old-fashioned ship for her time, was a thing of beauty, a source of pride for all of Clydeside.

The 1950s were part of the era when going 'Doon the Watter' to Dunoon or Rothesay for the Glasgow Fair was still an institution. Certainly, people were beginning to look further afield when it came to holidays; but the decade remained a boom time for the Clyde. The summers of 1955 and 1959 in particular were memorably hot, and the Clyde steamers benefited from the demand for their services. On a Glasgow Fair Saturday in the 1950s, thousands of holidaymakers would leave the city by steamer.

By the late 1960s and into the 1970s, as a result of social and economic changes, Scots were more able to take holidays on the continent. Demand in the Clyde estuary, as elsewhere, was for car ferries rather than pleasure boats.

CalMac ferry. Reproduced with kind permission of Caledonian MacBrayne Ltd.

Reproduced with kind permission of Caledonian MacBrayne Ltd.

Getting into a raincoat and braving a downpour on the decks of a paddle steamer began to seem mildly eccentric when you could take a plane to instant sunshine.

The shipping companies that formed Caledonian MacBrayne had been established in the nineteenth century as steamship companies (see Chapter 4, 'The People's Ocean'), but the prime interest of Caledonian MacBrayne in the 1970s was in taking passengers – most of them with their cars, although there was also some excursion trade – from point A to point B. The *Waverley*, with her spacious open deck, was confined to summer pleasure-sailing. Her future at this point looked as black as the livery on her funnel. John Whittle, former executive director of CalMac, takes up the story:

CalMac ferry. Reproduced with kind permission of Caledonian MacBrayne Ltd.

She was the last passenger steamer on the Clyde but was increasingly uneconomic to run. It became clear that trying to get people away from their cars was like trying to cut their arm off. Although she had to be laid up in winter, a big expense, the *Waverley* was still a very attractive ship and brought in a lot of custom. Sadly, by 1973, it was decided that we could not continue with her. By this point, we had two ships doing excursions and we took the view that we could only support one. We had to choose between the *Queen Mary* and the *Waverley*. The *Waverley*'s boilers were suspect at that time, and the *Queen Mary* had undergone a recent refit. She was a more economical ship to run, a bigger carrier, so we decided to dispose of the *Waverley*. Normally, with any other ship, having taken that decision we would have put her on the market and in this case she would have gone for scrap; there wouldn't have been an operational role for her anywhere else. But we felt it was totally wrong for the *Waverley*. We didn't want her turned into razor blades. She's unique, she's the last of a long and proud line of paddle steamers, part of the national heritage; a very, very special ship. At that time, there had been talk of a maritime museum, but that fizzled out so we kept looking around for ways in which she could be preserved. Fortunately, we had a very good relationship with the Paddle Steamer Preservation Society, and I suggested to Douglas McGowan of the organisation that they might get involved. After he recovered from the shock, he consulted his friends and they decided to take her on. They've done a marvellous job.

(BBC interview 2003)

The Scottish branch of the Paddle Steamer Preservation Society (PSPS) had been up and running since the late 1960s and they were very active in trying to preserve the paddle steamer *Caledonia*. Later, they turned their attention to saving the *Waverley*. She was sold by Caledonian MacBrayne to the PSPS for a token payment of £1 in 1973, the same year that Caledonian MacBrayne was formed.

However, many thought that even if she could be preserved it would not be as a working ship but as a static feature. These same people, however, are the first to express delight at the way in which interest in Scotland's maritime heritage has given the *Waverley* a new – and active – lease of life. Alan Jamieson again:

*Waverley's funnels.
Reproduced with
kind permission of
Waverley Excursions Ltd.*

Captaining this ship is the fulfilment of an ambition, a bit of a
dream really. I came from tramp ships, coasters, but when the
opportunity came I didn't hesitate. The *Waverley* is a typical paddle
steamer – she has her foibles, her rudder is a little bit small, so
she has a large turning circle for a vessel of her size. But she does
what she was designed to do, which was to move fast through the
water – quick acceleration on and off the berth. There's a popular
misconception that all paddle steamers are easy to manoeuvre.
They're anything but. A lot of people think you can put one paddle
ahead and another astern, which would turn the ship around on
its own length. But this vessel has a single shaft, two fixed paddles
on either side and so that doesn't work; it only drives ahead, and
that's why the ship has a turning circle of about a quarter of a
mile. The recent refurbishment has extended the life of the ship
considerably. It means that the new generation, the youngsters,
brought by their parents, can come on board and see a traditional
vessel. What you see is not just a preserved ship. There are a lot
of seafaring skills in evidence here on a daily basis that sadly are
dying out. It's also true that there is a special rhythm to the paddles.
I was waiting at Greenock one day for my colleague coming over
from Helensburgh, and I heard him as soon as he started leaving
the pier. I could hear the beat of the paddles. I heard them increase
the speed, six miles away. It's a lovely, quiet, steady throb – reliable.
What it says to me is reliability.

(BBC interview 2003)

Reproduced with kind permission of Waverley Excursions Ltd.

Today, a team of volunteers and paid employees runs the *Waverley*. Her upkeep is enormously expensive, and in recent years the project has received £7m from the Heritage Lottery Commission. The *Waverley* 'clan' of enthusiasts, with support from other organisations such as Argyll and Bute Council and Glasgow City Council, managed to raise about £2m, which allowed the heritage lottery cash to start flowing. With daily running costs for the ship and her infrastructure estimated at a staggering £8,500–£9,000, the cash-raising effort has to be powerful and sustained.

Recently, the *Waverley* has been restored from bow to stern, although pieces of machinery on the bridge and in the engine room have simply been overhauled. For example, the original 1947 steering gear made by Brown Brothers of Edinburgh is still in place and intact, the only changes being some manufactured spare parts. Says Alan Jamieson:

Reproduced with kind permission of Waverley Excursions Ltd.

> You don't buy spare parts for a vessel like this off the shelf. You make them. I think it's a great tribute to the men of Clydeside who constructed this ship that it's lasted so long. If it hadn't been properly built in the first place, it wouldn't be here today.

In fact, she has been restored to a higher standard than her original specifications and, given continued support from the public walking down the gangway for a cruise, and enthusiasts giving of their own time and effort, the future looks bright.

Another major element in her continuing success, apart from the endless dedication of the enthusiasts who have kept her in business, is her original design. Iain Quinn, tour guide on the ship, explains:

> An important point about the paddle steamers is that they have a shallow draught. They can go in and out of small ports and harbours where bigger tonnage couldn't. That, effectively, is what makes the *Waverley* work today. We can nick into all these wee ports and piers that have very little water. She can pick up people and away we go. That's what she was built to do.
>
> (BBC interview 2003)

Organising the annual timetable is a complex and time-consuming aspect of the winter lay-up. The ship calls in at more than 100 ports, and everything has to fit together like a jigsaw. In addition, much loving care is given to the machinery during the winter months to have her up and ready for the new season.

Iain Quinn is a paddle-steamer enthusiast who has had a thirty-year love affair with the ship. His father was a professional seaman, and his grandmother had a house in Dunoon – a combination of circumstances that perhaps helps explain Iain's passion. He remembers:

> In the 1970s, when we were staying with granny at Dunoon, it was obvious that the Clyde steamer was going to become a thing of the past. The ships I saw fascinated me. There was the *Queen Mary*, which was a turbine; the *Waverley*, of course; the *Caledonia*, which was another paddle-ship; and the *Duchess of Hamilton*, also a turbine – two paddles and two turbines.

Reproduced with kind permission of Waverley Excursions Ltd.

The Waverley. *Reproduced with kind permission of Waverley Excursions Ltd.*

Iain has no doubt as to what creates the *Waverley*'s special magic. He believes that the visitors bring the ship to life. When the season starts at Easter, the steam goes through the ship, the people climb aboard; he can sense a good trip ahead. He believes that today's sightseers are there for the journey rather than the destination, and he sees it as his duty to try to help people understand what Clyde steaming was really like in its heyday. That so many people have been persuaded to leave their cars behind for twenty-first-century trip 'doon the watter' speaks volumes about both the magic of the *Waverley* and the effort put in by her dedicated supporters.

Waiting on the *Robert E. Lee*

Shortly after the outbreak of the American Civil War, in 1861, the Confederacy, foreseeing a serious shortfall in weapons and munitions, sent secret agents to the Clyde in search of fast ships. Already in place across the United Kingdom – in ports such as Liverpool, Bristol, Glasgow and London – was a network of Federal spies. They monitored the construction, launch and despatch of vessels destined for Confederate blockade-running, and they were able to give the Federal navy department detailed descriptions of the ships that were on their way.

The British government declared itself neutral in the American Civil War, and Queen Victoria issued a proclamation requesting that her loyal subjects should not break the blockade which the Federal navy had placed around the major Confederate ports down the eastern seaboard. However, the southern states at that time supplied about 70 per cent of the world's cotton – and, as hundreds

hundreds of of British mills depended on that trade, a major crisis loomed. In the first year of the war, the flow of cotton stopped almost completely, and mills began to close. Many people in Lancashire and the Manchester area lost their jobs, and many went hungry. Not surprisingly, British cotton manufacturers saw an urgent need to reinstate the flow of cotton. Bob Thorp, whose great-great-grandfather was a blockade runner, explains:

> Britain turned a blind eye, really, to the whole business of assisting the Confederacy, primarily because we needed the commerce. A blind eye was also turned to the so-called commerce 'raiders' that we were building in British shipyards because they were getting rid of competition by sinking Yankee ships. That whole episode basically put Britain back in supremacy in commerce shipping.

> (BBC interview 2003)

A company in the port of Liverpool called Fraser, Trenholm and Co. was one of the main traders with Charleston, South Carolina, and they clandestinely acted as bankers for the Confederacy so that their agents could go around buying ships, guns and ammunition with the credit the company offered.

In 1862, the Confederate agents turned their attention to the Clyde estuary, where they had received reports of excellent steamships ideally suited for buying and sending across the Atlantic as blockade-runners. They were looking for fast, nimble, little ships with a shallow draught, characteristics for which the Clyde steamers were famed. Typically, the Clyde-built steamships could do

Detail from Com. Farragut's fleet, passing the forts on the Mississippi, 24 April 1862. Getty Images. See back endpaper for the full picture.

between fifteen and eighteen knots, whereas most of the blockading ships could manage only ten or twelve knots. Compared with some of the cargo ships, the Clyde steamers were relatively small and so were unable to carry much cargo. However, they could run the blockade by operating in shallow river estuaries where the blockade ships did not dare follow. The first Clyde boat to be taken into the trade was the *Herald*, which had been operating for the Glasgow & Dublin Steam Packet Company. One of the most celebrated blockade runners was the *Robert E. Lee*. She was built on the Clyde and she started life modestly as the *Giraffe*, carrying mail from Glasgow to Belfast.

The Clyde steamships that found their way into the American Civil War had typically been used on rivers or for coastal trade and were not designed for deep-ocean running. To take these ships across the Atlantic, on routes that allowed for re-coaling at far-flung places such as Madeira, the Azores and the Canary Islands, was a hazardous enterprise. The ships had auxiliary sails so that the easterly winds and currents could carry them across the ocean, usually making landfall in Puerto Rico where, after a further refuelling stop, they would head north into the war zone.

Cargoes of arms, ammunitions and general supplies were taken across the Atlantic in larger ships that were too cumbersome and slow to attempt to run the blockade. At ports such as Nassau in the Bahamas, Bermuda, and Havana in Cuba, the goods would be broken down into smaller consignments and transferred to the Clyde steamers. They would then make their sprint to the eastern seaboard. The Clyde paddle steamers were very successful at this work.

The blockade-runners took in almost every conceivable product to the beleaguered Southern ports. Most of the skippers and crews were not in that dangerous business for altruistic reasons, but purely for profit. After safe landfall, they would charge exorbitant prices as they sold on the goods and weapons.

Altogether, there were about 300 steamers in the trade, of which about forty were actually owned by the Confederacy. At one time, it was said that there were 100 Clyde-built steamers operating in the fleet of blockade-busters.

The staple exchange was cotton, tobacco and kerosene going out to pay for the ships, and ammunition coming in. During the last six months of 1864, the blockade-runners imported around 1,500 tons of meat, 800 tons of lead for making bullets and 500 tons of saltpetre for manufacturing gunpowder.

The risks for the blockade-runners were obvious. They were confronting a well-organised and well-equipped navy, so some men were killed and many were captured. In the case of a British national being captured, deportation was the likely outcome. The Federal navy was anxious not to create international incidents by imprisoning the seamen of another nation. Any Confederates on

Tactics for running the blockade

The blockade ring was usually set up across the entrance to the main rivers and harbours of the eastern-seaboard cities, which the Federal government was trying to starve into submission. In any one blockade, there might be as many as twenty ships guarding a particular inlet. The biggest problem for the commanders in charge of the blockade was that the crews became bored by this sentry duty and their attention would wander, allowing ships through – sometimes even in daylight. However, most attempts to break the blockade were made in the dead of night, preferably a moonless night. The sound of nearby breakers would cover the noise of the paddles. The steamships would have the entire superstructure, apart from the wheelhouse, stripped off to make the ship low in profile. They were painted grey, a precursor of the grey camouflage of modern warships. The blockade-runners would hug the coast and, making full use of their shallow draught, attempt to squeeze between the shore and the last warship in the blockade line. If they were spotted, they were in trouble, because the blockade-runners were unarmed and the blockade ships were generally bristling with guns. All sorts of tricks were employed to beat the blockade. One blockade-running skipper would run up the Stars and Stripes and sit among the Federal vessels pretending to be part of the blockade, waiting for nightfall.

a captured blockade-runner were, of course, immediately taken into custody as prisoners-of-war.

Captain James Duguid delivered the *Robert E. Lee* to the Confederacy. Most of the time, he was based in the Bahamas and he ran the blockade into Wilmington, North Carolina. He was a very methodical individual who thought he had blockade-running down to a fine art. His great-great-grandson, Bob Thorp, explains:

> He always reckoned that the real risk lasted for about six minutes, so if you could get up full steam and just go hell for leather if you

were spotted, then you could usually get away from them. You'd be in range for six minutes. Probably an exaggeration, but there you go. The main defence was to make themselves almost invisible against the land and the line of breakers by being so low in the water. They quite often boasted that they could get to within 100 yards of a blockader and still not be seen at night.

James Duguid became involved in the Civil War because he had married into the Liverpool shipbuilding family of William Cowley Miller & Sons. They had been contracted by the Confederates to build a warship. Originally, an American skipper had been pencilled in to take the ship across the Atlantic; but he was doing so much sterling work in procuring other warships in the United Kingdom that it was decided to retain his services in Britain. Who better to replace him than the son-in-law of the man who had built the ship? That was how James Alexander Duguid, whose father had been pressganged into the navy in Scotland during the Napoleonic Wars, got involved, delivering the ship to the Confederate navy in Nassau. It left Liverpool as the *Orito* and went into war service renamed the CSS *Florida*. Once James was on the payroll, he was commissioned several times to make deliveries.

The story of the Giraffe

After James Duguid had delivered the **Orito** and returned to Liverpool, he was immediately asked by the Confederacy to take out a Clyde steamer called the **Giraffe**, which had been used as a mail steamer between Glasgow and Belfast. Purchased for £32,000, she was a very fast and classy steamer and was delivered by Duguid to the Confederate navy at Wilmington in North Carolina. As was their habit, the Confederates renamed her the **Robert E. Lee**, and she came under the command of one of the most famous Confederate skippers, John Wilkinson. The **Robert E. Lee** was eventually captured by the Union, renamed **Fort Donelson** and, ironically, used as a blockader against the blockade-runners. Her fortune had turned full circle. She was a classic example of poacher turned gamekeeper. Another Clyde-built ship taken over by James Duguid was the **Juno**, which was used as a harbour patrol boat in Charleston but which sank in an Atlantic storm.

Captain Eric Walford.

Captain Duguid was described by some as a hero and by others as a pirate, but he was, without question, an extremely skilled mariner. He had been at sea since he was fourteen years old and was naval-trained, so he knew what to expect from the warships in terms of manoeuvring and how to get past a warship without allowing its guns to be brought to bear on his ship.

According to Bob Thorp, his antecedent was far from squeaky clean. He was a bit of a rogue; a rascal in fact. Before the Civil War, he had been the captain of a so-called 'coffin' ship running distressed emigrants from the Irish potato famine across to Canada and returning with a cargo of timber. Most historians now agree that it was a very lucrative trade for some not-too-honest ship-owners. Says Bob:

I think blockade-running suited him down to the ground. He thought it was a great game. He was one of the most successful blockade-runners of the war, skipping the blockade twenty-one times. In addition, he retired a rich man – and uncaught.

The paddlers at war

The American Civil War was not the only conflict in which the Clyde steamers performed well. In 1942, Captain Eric Walford was serving as a Royal Navy Volunteer Reserve (RNVR) sub-lieutenant on the paddle steamer HMS *Jeanie Deans*, but was desperate to see some service on what he described as a more 'war-like vessel'.

In Eric Walford's eyes, the paddle steamers went nowhere, merely going out to sea and dropping anchor, swinging round it for twenty-four hours and then coming back. There were no patrols or U-boat-hunting, and even the enemy aircraft were not interested in them. Eric recalled:

I wanted a real ship. I wanted destroyers. When I first got my commission and put down a preference, I put down destroyers. The old paddle steamers weren't bad. They could nearly all do fifteen knots, although the *Jeanie Deans* was reputed to be able to do nineteen knots. But what I really wanted was to thrash around if necessary at thirty knots, banging off guns at a real target.

(BBC interview 2003)

While the *Jeanie Deans* was in Chatham naval dockyard to have her boiler cleaned, Eric took the opportunity to go to the Admiralty and request – or in his own words to 'beg, beseech and bribe' – a posting on one of the Navy's fleet of destroyers rather than on a paddle steamer. Back came a letter saying that he had been appointed to HMS *Ryde* and that he was to make his way to HMS *Wildfire* at Sheerness. Eric explained how he eventually reached his new posting:

> I spent the night at HMS *Wildfire* and made some inquiries, but nobody seemed too sure exactly what the *Ryde* was. Anyway, I was told to take a boat that ran out to all the ships, like a bus, and there she was. The *Ryde* was another paddle steamer! I climbed aboard, introduced myself, and as I looked around I thought: 'Somebody up there doesn't love me'. However, I decided that I would have to make the best of a bad job.

Eric Walford realised that it would be a waste of time to go to the Admiralty to seek another posting, but he found that the *Ryde* was a happy ship and one for which he had great affection. She was built by Denny's of Dumbarton and belonged to the Southern Railway, operating the short haul from Portsmouth to Ryde on the Isle of Wight. She carried only one anchor and only seventy tons of coal. Coaling on the *Ryde* was a nightmare. The coal was stored behind the bridge and had to be fed down a manhole to the deck below, from where it was shovelled down another deck to the hold. The dust went everywhere. According to Eric:

HMS Ryde. *With permission of Portsmouth Museums and Records Service.*

> ### Minesweeping duties
>
> *Paddle steamers in the Second World War took on the role of auxiliary minesweepers. Lacking sophisticated equipment, the steamers used a sweep wire which cut the tethers mooring the mines. The mines then bobbed up and were destroyed by gunfire. The extra payments made to minesweeper crews reflected the dangers that the Admiralty felt were faced by these men.*

It didn't matter. You turned the fans off, you closed your portholes, everything like that, but after you coaled the ship everything had taken on a layer of coal dust, everything. We used to be envious of other ships where they just connected a pipe and pumped in fuel oil. Made us spit, that did. Yes, the coaling was a dreadful business.

There is no doubt that the Clyde paddle steamers made an important contribution to the war effort, even simply as anti-aircraft ships. Captain Walford recalled a cartoon during the war which depicted an American troopship, full of American soldiers and bristling with guns, and in the corner there was a paddle steamer with a few guns and a couple of sailors leaning over the side of the troopship, one saying to the other: 'We're safe now, Jake, our escort's arrived!'

It is estimated that, as well as their role in the Normandy landings, paddle steamers managed to evacuate 26,000 troops after France was overrun by German forces in 1940. The paddle steamers drew only six feet of water, and, even at the risk of wrecking the bow rudder, the skippers would take them right in until the bow rested on the sand and the troops could climb aboard directly from the shore. The only problem that arose was when the ship swung parallel to the shore, risking grounding.

Destroyers, on the other hand, might have drawn fourteen feet and could get nowhere near the tide line. The paddle steamers could accommodate far more men, perhaps up to 2,000, because they were built for that very purpose. Destroyers already had a crew of 300 and, with the upper deck space crammed with torpedo tubes, guns, winches and boats, they were full and overflowing, taking only half as many evacuees as the paddle steamers.

Four sailors were needed to drag a man from the water on to a destroyer: two were needed to climb down the net to the water and help the half-drowned, waterlogged victim up towards the deck, where another two men would be at the top to help. This, as many Dunkirk veterans were able to testify, was exhausting work. Aboard the paddle steamers, on the other hand, there were ladders on the paddle-wheel covers that could be lowered into the water to make the climb to safety easier. In many ways, with their acres of deck space, the paddle steamers were ideal for such a rescue mission. They were joined in bringing men to safety at the water margin by the famous fleet of little boats while the larger warships were compelled to stand offshore waiting for the men to be ferried out to them.

Captain Walford had some very forthright views about the need to preserve these older vessels rather than leaving them to rot in some backwater, a fate he found infinitely sad:

> These ships, including the paddle steamers, are relics of our past, of a time when we were a great people, which we aren't now. You see, we've forgotten what we could do, what we did do. I've been in the Far East, and I think: 'How on earth did sailing ships get there and back home again – no radar, no shore lights, no echo-sounder, nothing?' It is just a miracle that they managed it.

Shortly after being interviewed for *The Scots at Sea*, Captain Eric Walford died in the Philippines.

Puffing down the Clyde

It will come as a great surprise to many to learn that landlocked Kirkintilloch, on the Forth and Clyde Canal in East Dunbartonshire, was once one of Scotland's great shipbuilding centres. More significantly, it was the world capital of the construction of puffers – plucky little steam cargo boats immortalised in Neil Munro's tales of *Para Handy* and in the sentimental Ealing movie *The Maggie*.

Before the advent of the railways in the early nineteenth century, canals were the major form of inland transport. It was even possible to book a berth on a 'sleeper boat' between Grangemouth and Glasgow. In the 1840s, the train network was developing, and the canals needed to innovate and replace the horse-drawn barges with something more efficient.

The first puffer appeared in the 1850s with the conversion of a canal barge, the *Thomas*, to steam propulsion. The original puffers were always approximately sixty-seven feet long so that they could fit snugly into the canal locks. However,

the vessels were unable to flourish until the development of the screw propeller because their paddles protruded too far. Canal owners were worried about the potential damage to the canal banks as the early vessels steamed along at five miles per hour.

Described poetically as the 'work-horse of the west', the Clyde puffer was in its later years often the target for ridicule, perceived as a refuge for eccentric, hard-living old salts. However, its arrival in the late 1850s transformed life for people on the islands and in isolated lochside communities up and down the west coast. Lifeline transport links to these more remote outposts had always been difficult until the puffers took over the job. For more than a century, they carried building materials, coal and timber. Every time a house was built in the islands, a puffer would deliver the materials almost to the doorstep. Foodstuffs, mail, livestock, fuel and people generally arrived by ferry.

The puffers also performed occasional duties such as servicing the whisky industry by bringing the barrels of spirit out from far-flung distilleries. They also acted as 'lighters', service vessels for the liners that used the Clyde estuary.

Originally designed for work on the canals, the first true version of this legendary vessel was built at Swan's Yard in Maryhill, Glasgow, in 1857. Early puffers had their exhausts drawn back up through the funnel to help the boiler fire to draw. Puffs of smoke kept rhythmic time with the piston, while the noise of the exhaust earned them their nickname. They were launched broadside into the canal from several boatbuilding yards, notably at Kirkintilloch and Maryhill.

By the 1870s, the puffers had taken over the West Highland trade, making it more reliable. People on the islands would organise themselves into coal clubs so that they could collectively buy a cargo of coal – perhaps taking a ton each on arrival in the islands. Puffers were used extensively during the First World War at Rosyth, Scapa Flow and Invergordon. By this time, however, the improving road network was already beginning to threaten the puffer trade. The Second World War really marked the end of the era of the steam puffer when diesel came into vogue – a less labour-intensive and cleaner source of propulsion than coal.

Built with a shallow draught, the puffers were manoeuvrable and could be beached – with a bit of skilful seamanship – at far-flung locations lacking a pier. Loading and unloading cargoes such as coal was always heavy work. At

Portrait of a puffer

The puffer **Spartan** was built in 1942 by Hay & Sons of Kirkintilloch for war service. She was No. 18 of the VICs (Victualling Inshore Craft). The Admiralty looked at various designs before deciding that the puffer suited its needs best. After the war, the VIC fleet was sold off, and Hay's (who also ran a puffer fleet) bought her back and registered the vessel as **Spartan** on 24 September 1946. She was the third of the Hay's fleet to carry that name, continuing their tradition of naming vessels after peoples or tribes. Other vessels owned by them were called **Saxon**, **Celt**, **Briton**, **Trojan** and **Slav**. **Spartan** was soon employed in carrying coal and general cargoes as far as Mull, Iona and Islay. In 1959, the continuing decline of the coasting trade encouraged Hays to convert their fleet to diesel power for efficiency, and **Spartan** was fitted with a Scania diesel engine in 1961. She continued to work for Hay's and their successors, the Glenlight Shipping Company, until 1980 when she was laid up at Bowling. In 1982, she was acquired by a group of enthusiasts, the West of Scotland Boat Museum Association, and became the focus of the nascent Scottish Maritime Museum, set up in Irvine in 1983. An ever-popular exhibit, she has taken part in classic ship gatherings and starred in the 1990s series of **Para Handy** tales as the **Golden Star**. She is included in the 'designated' list of the National Historic Ships Committee.

the remote beaches, goods would be unloaded with the help of the islanders or villagers, and then the puffer crew would await high tide.

By the late nineteenth century, technology had advanced sufficiently to see three variants of the puffer out on the water. These were the 'inside' boat, used only for canal or dock work; the 'shorehead' boat, which worked the estuaries; and the 'outside' boat, which was the version that quickly became a familiar sight along the western seaboard of Scotland. Famous among these were the *Vital Spark* – real name the *Saxon* – built at Hay's yard in Kirkintilloch, and the *Inca* and the *Boer*, both of which featured in *The Maggie*.

For the men on board, living was cramped: accommodation comprised cabins aft of the engine room. Normally, the puffers carried a crew of four – the skipper, engineer, mate and deck boy. There was a strict hierarchy, and

Scene from The Vital Spark.

everyone was expected to turn their hand to anything. Tommy Ferguson worked the puffers for thirty-three years and remembers the gradual process of learning the ropes:

> Everyone joined the puffer as a cook or deckhand, and you learned everything. Nothing was missed out. You learned the basics until you became mate. You took this knowledge in, and it stayed there because it had to stay there. In those days, we had no radar, we had nothing – only a compass. All the lights, all the courses stayed in your head. You always kept a book for beaching puffers. This book would maybe say: 'Keep the two telegraph poles in line as you come in and don't go on the beach until half an hour after high water or you might not get back off'. All these things were learned over a number of years. Nobody made skipper straight away.

> (BBC interview 2003)

Beach books were a skipper's Bible. Often there were no piers or roads where the puffers were headed, and the cargoes had to be delivered as near to the community as possible. This is when beaching was necessary and the puffer with its shallow draught came into its own. Landing a craft in this way called on an intricate knowledge of tides, currents and bays; it was information gleaned over decades and passed on from captain to captain. It was still practised on Iona until the 1980s. The common practice was to take the puffer as far inshore

Tommy Ferguson.

as possible on the high tide. As the tide went out, it lowered the vessel on to the beach, and the cargo was offloaded. Beaching was always a risky business: getting the phasing of the moon wrong could see a puffer marooned for up to a fortnight. Loading and unloading was heavy work but did occasion the odd laugh, as Tommy Ferguson recalls:

> Working round the islands really made you feel as if you were part of the islands. You were welcomed. You weren't a tourist. They liked to see you. The cargo we carried was anything from complete houses to coal, steel, tarry metal for the roads, building materials, occasionally some sheep, cows … When the farmer was there, he'd put them down the hold, but it was usually left to us. Quite often, we'd be told to put the cattle ashore and the boys would be down the hold chasing the Highland cows with their big horns, trying to get belts round them, shouting: 'That one's pregnant, better watch that one'. It was quite exciting – you were farmer as well as sailor half the time.

Today, the localised knowledge gained by these sailors has started to fade. By the 1990s, like many of Scotland's treasured vessels, the puffers had succumbed to the inevitable. Competition from road transport and large 'roll-on-roll-off' ferries was just too great. As day trips to the Western Isles gave way to touring in the car, so the puffers were overtaken by the heavy goods vehicle.

Len Paterson, former chairman of Glenlight Shipping Company, believes this has had a devastating impact:

SS Zephon. *With kind permission of Len Paterson.*

I think there was a short-sightedness about sea transport in the government of that particular day. I always saw the puffers as being complementary to the sort of services CalMac and Western Ferries were providing ... we did the bulk cargoes and they did the

Still going strong

A number of the old puffers are still to the fore:

- The 1943 English-built puffer VIC32 is now a passenger/leisure craft based at Crinan. She is owned by Nick and Rachel Walker, who began restoring her in 1975.

- **Auld Reekie** (VIC27), of 1943 vintage, is also based at Crinan.

- **Pibroch** (1956) is the second boat of this name. She is owned by the White Horse distillery in Islay.

- The only Scottish-built VIC puffer, the **Spartan** (formerly VIC18), dating back to 1942, can be seen at the Scottish Maritime Museum, Irvine.

passengers and the light cargoes and the holidaymakers and things like that ... The environmental impact of losing the puffers was to throw everything on to the roads, and that has serious consequences for the cost of the roads themselves and for the cost of getting materials to the islanders, because they can only get in twenty-ton lots instead of 120. So, there's a whole hidden subsidy there. Never mind pollution, never mind noise; different departments pay for different things, and the total cost of road transport as distinct from sea transport for the Western Isles is lost. Fossil fuels are not getting cheaper, taxes on fossil fuels are going up, so what we've done to the least economically successful area in Scotland is give it the most inefficient, uneconomic form of transport.

(BBC interview 2003)

Glenlight Shipping ended its last cargo run to the Western Isles in 1993. The lifeline services that so inspired Neil Munro and a legion of fans remain consigned to history and the pages of fiction.

SS Spartan. *With kind permission of Len Paterson.*

PUBLISHED BY CURRIER & IVES,

FORT ST. PHILIP.   BURNING RAFTS.   FORT JACKSON.

Entered according to act of Congress, in the year 1862, by Currier & Ives, in the Clerk

COM. FARRAGUT'S FLEET, PASSING TH

The U.S. Frigate Mississippi de